WITHDRAWN

THE POWER OF DANTE

THE POWER OF DANTE

BY

C. H. GRANDGENT, L.H.D.

CORRESPONDING MEMBER OF THE ACCADEMIA DELLA CRUSCA
PROFESSOR OF ROMANCE LANGUAGES IN HARVARD UNIVERSITY

BOSTON
MARSHALL JONES COMPANY
MDCCCCXVIII

THE UNIVERSITY PRESS, CAMBRIDGE, U. S. A.

PREFACE

THIS book consists of a series of eight lectures delivered at the Lowell Institute in the autumn of 1917. They are here presented substantially as they were pronounced; but I have reinforced them, in some of the thinner places, with material drawn from a course on "The Artistry of Dante" given by me in the early months of 1918 at Yale University.

The translations are my own. While most of them are new, some are borrowed from works already in print. For permission to use the latter I am indebted to the courtesy of Duffield & Co., publishers of my *Dante* (New York, 1916), and the Harvard University Press, which published *The Ladies of Dante's Lyrics* (Cambridge, 1917).

C. H. G.

CAMBRIDGE, June 6, 1918.

CONTENTS

THE POWER OF DANTE

LECTURE I

FAITH

WHY am I here to-day, lecturing about a man who died some six hundred years ago? Why are other lecturers, to-day and wellnigh every day, discoursing of the same man, so long departed, and why are people listening to them, in so many different lands? Why does the press pour forth, year after year, such a flood of books and articles on Dante that it would require a specialist's whole time merely to keep track of them? Why does one man of letters bring out a volume on references to Dante in English literature, while another writes a thick tome on Dante in France? Why, during the last century, have so many eminent men in various walks of life — not only the poet, the scholar, the critic, but the priest, the jurist, the king — been drawn irresistibly to devote their best energies to the increase or the diffusion of knowledge of this same ancient Florentine? Why — to pass from proofs obvious and tangible to testimony at once more intimate and more significant — do so many thousands of men and women at this very day, — many of them dwellers in lands far remote from Italy, many of them nearly ignorant even of Dante's tongue, — still find in his writings a spell which binds them ever closer, a solace which comforts when all other consolation fails? What, in other words, is the source of Dante's enduring power? What has given him such a mighty hold on humanity, a grip that time seems only to strengthen? To answer in some part these questions is the purpose of this series of lectures.

Dante is not a recent discovery. His power began while he was still alive, and has lasted ever since. To be sure, it was somewhat obscured for several centuries, but it was never lost; and for the last hundred or hundred and fifty years it has waxed almost continuously. Commentaries on the *Divine Comedy* began appearing almost before the poem was finished, and every few years thereafter saw a new one. Within half a century or so of the poet's death a Dante professorship was established in Florence, and its first incumbent was no less a personage than Boccaccio. Petrarch complained that all sorts of ignorant people were continually reciting passages of the *Divine Comedy*, as even illiterate Italians do still.

Now, all the admirers of Dante are not attracted by the same things. Our poet was a many-sided genius, who has a message for nearly everyone. In his own time I believe he was most admired — at least by the educated class — for qualities that are now, in the judgment of the general run of readers, among the less attractive.

Certainly he was in the fourteenth century revered as a great teacher, a mine of philosophical and theological lore. Like Virgil, his master, he came to be regarded as the wisest man of his epoch, a prodigy of recondite learning. Like Virgil, too, he was even supposed by some to be a sorcerer, an imputation to which, in those days, any extraordinary scholar was liable. Learned and wise he truly was; an indefatigable student, eager to impart to mankind his hard-won stores; a close and subtle thinker, with a strong bent for abstract doctrine; an accomplished astronomer, fond of setting his reader intricate scientific puzzles. But all this erudition and speculation, which appealed so mightily to the utilitarian and argumentative spirit of his contemporaries and immediate followers, usually appears to modern readers dry and tiresome, and much of it is skipped by the profane. We are utilitarian enough, to be sure; but the greater part of Dante's erudition has lost its immediate utility, and most of his philosophy seems to the uninitiated to be out of key with present-day modes of thought.

Virgil and Ovid were, in Dante's day, held in high repute as allegorists, and were eagerly studied for the intricate hidden lessons that might be extracted from their verses. Dante really *was* an allegorist, and as such was justly esteemed. But his early commentators read into his work, as into that of Ovid and Virgil, all sorts of minute secondary meanings that were not there. Just as Christian preachers, from time immemorial, have

[3]

given to separate verses in the Bible any significance that might at the moment suit their fancy, so Dante expositors have found in single phrases and incidents of their author whatever their particular hobby suggested. This practice has continued, both for the Bible and for the *Divine Comedy*, down to our own day. But in the fourteenth century the interpretations of both books nearly always took an allegorical turn. At present, generally speaking, we care little for allegory, which, when it does not bore us, puzzles and baffles us. Probably few modern readers of Dante are really interested in his symbolism, except in its broadest outlines.

Two attributes, then, which fascinated Dante's contemporaries — utility and symbolic inventiveness — have lost a large portion of their spell. But there are enough left; and some of them, no doubt, are more effective to-day than they were six hundred years ago. His uncompromising faith and his rigid code of morals have now become so rare as to assume the interest of strangeness, whereas in the author's own era they were matters of course. His pronounced temperament is probably more appreciated in our epoch of aggressive individualism than in his own communal age. The course of his life, which furnished him with the experience that he translated into poetry, seems nowadays extraordinarily diversified, but was normal enough then. The clearness and comprehensiveness of both his physical and his intellectual sight are a wonder fit to appeal potently to the fourteenth century as to the twentieth; possibly the twentieth, which has been schooled by a long series of intervening talents to follow the higher flights of the imagination, contemplates this wonder more intelligently than did the fourteenth. As to the deep symbolism of his primal conception, and the unparalleled unity and symmetry with which he developed it, I am inclined to think that, on the whole, the fourteenth century readers were more competent judges than the twentieth century public; partly because, having far less to read than the people of our day, they read more closely and thoughtfully; partly because symbolism and symmetry were ever before them, mystic symbolism as the basis of their religious service and their whole outlook on the world, richly diversified symmetry as the underlying principle of their eccleciastical architecture at a time when the church was the one great meeting-place of the community. On the other hand, I believe that the really sympathetic specialist of to-day comprehends the poet's conception more clearly than did the best qualified specialist of the *Trecento;* I believe that Longfellow, Charles Eliot Norton, Edward Moore, alien though they were in race, time, and faith, grasped Dante's fundamental idea more closely than did Boccaccio or Benvenuto da Imola, the reason being that the modern interpreters possessed a broader experience in literature and had at their disposal the results of centuries of study of their author. Dante's technical skill — his use of harmony and contrast,

[5]

suspense, surprise, climax, of metaphor and simile, his choice of words — was as astounding to his age as it is to ours; even more astounding, because it was then something quite unprecedented in modern literature. Though Dante as a craftsman is still unsurpassed, he has in the course of six centuries found a few fellows; in his own day he had none nearer than Virgil and Ovid, who were thirteen hundred years away.

It is to these elements of Dante's power that I intend to devote my eight lectures: Faith, Morality, Temperament, Experience, Vision, Conception, Workmanship, Diction. I hope by the discussion of these themes, and especially by the citation of illustrative passages from the author hmself, to throw some light on the secret of the lasting poetic supremacy of a man who not only lived six hundred years ago, but distinctly belonged to his own epoch — an epoch whose ideas and interests seem so remote from ours.

Before I enter upon the subject of Faith, which is to be my text to-day, I must make one more preliminary remark. I spoke, a moment ago, of the diverse habits of reading in the Middle Ages and now. Remember this: Dante must be read in the medieval way. He must be read slowly (if possible, aloud), intently, ponderingly, repeatedly. Whosoever tries to speed through him as one rushes through the season's best seller, gets nothing, or next to nothing. We have almost lost the art of reading. So prodigious is the mass of printed matter which year by year, month by month, day by day, obtrudes itself on our attention, and with which we feel in some fashion obliged to acquire at least a semblance of familiarity, that we have formed the habit of skimming, of leaping from peak to peak, instead of following the road up hill and down dale; and honest, thorough perusal has for most of us become nearly inpossible. Chief blame for our mental degeneracy falls on the daily paper, — I say nothing of the Sunday paper, which contains no news and therefore need corrupt only those willing to be corrupted, — but the daily paper, which we have to examine, to learn what is going on in the world, — the daily paper, which, with its preposterous bulk, its interminable long-windedness, its chaotic arrangement, forces us to practice every day for an hour or so a system of violent intellectual gymastics adopted by us for the purpose of winnowing the few grains of corn which we assume to be there from the enormous mass of chaff which we know is there. That is, we engage every day on a struggle to extricate from a formless and mostly void heap of print the few things we want while reading just as little as possible of the things that are of no interest. This method, slightly relaxed, we carry into our perusal of the weekly short-story periodical, to which we have been lured by the illustrations. With only a little diminution of tenseness, we apply it to the monthly magazine. Then, if we ever have time to read a book, the habit has become such a second nature that we find ourselves dodging from page to page, from chapter to chapter, breathless, cramped, un-enlightened, and unamused. How happy were the people of the Middle Ages, most of whom could not read at all, while those who possessed the art could devote an undisturbed lifetime to the five-foot shelf, studying their choice authors phrase by phrase, reflecting, turning back, unconsciously committing to memory — something as we (I mean those of us who have lived half a century and more) used in our childhood to peruse the Bible and Shakespeare and Dickens. The practice of real communion with an author, which until our own generation has been the chief delight and the chief education of cultivated people, has well-nigh disappeared. It can be restored only by a firm resolve, on the part of the seekers for light, to devote a certain portion of their week or their year to quiet concentration upon some writer whose unquestioned greatness is sure to repay them for the precious time thus spent. The tend-ency to half-attentive fleetness can be counter-acted in some measure by reading aloud. To me it seems — as it has seemed to many others, better judges than I — that among the authors who best reward such sacrifice Dante stands preëminent.

I may be mistaken, but I cannot help thinking that the same superficiality which vitiates our read-ing is apparent in our religion. I do not mean that most of those who profess religion (of course vast numbers nowadays make no such profession) are insincere. I mean that very generally their faith is not a constant, vital force in their lives,

[8]

FAITH

determining or at least influencing their every act and every thought. More and more we take our articles of belief in a Pickwickian sense, if we think of them at all; and when there comes among us a revivalist who really accepts in all literalness the dogmas to which he, in common with millions of others, has subscribed, he seems grotesque. And yet there is a very widespread craving for some absolute faith — a craving deep but usually unspoken, often unconscious. How many of our fellow countrymen, when cut adrift from their traditional religious support, are eager to clutch at any straw of supernatural comfort! How many strange, uncouth churches and sects have sprung up and flourished among us, testifying to a persistent hunger for the " bread of the angels," for spiritual teaching, for assured truth!

This underlying need is, I think, accountable, to some extent, for the strong reaction produced by the *Divine Comedy* on so many men who do not pass for religious. In Dante they see a great intelligence, admired for centuries, an absolutely authentic and undoubted genius, whose faith in the revealed word of God is unwavering, to whom the doctrines of his Church are even more real than the events and the people of this mortal world which he knew so well. Such an example is encouraging to one who longs for faith, yet has been checked by the suspicion that faith dwells with babes and simpletons alone. No one need fear shame at doing what a Dante did, or bowing to what a Dante revered, or worshiping as a

[9]

Dante prayed. Even to him who cannot believe, the spectacle of such a staunch believer is reassuring, especially if that believer be a man of evidently superior intellectual power. As to the reader who is already devout, he finds in Dante a fellow and a champion after his own heart, a comrade who corroborates his credence before his own eyes and justifies it in the eyes of others. Both to the religious and to the superficially irreligious our poet offers, then, the comfort of a stalwart faith.

No mental reservation impairs Dante's acceptance of divine authority. Not a backward look does he cast when he entrusts himself to its keeping. "No man, having put his hand to the plough, and looking back, is fit for the kingdom of God." When, on his allegorical journey, Dante reaches with Virgil, his guide, the gate of Purgatory, the angelic keeper warns the travelers of their danger:

> The angel pusht the sacred portal wide,
>   And said: " Now enter, but I caution you
>   That he who looks behind must go outside."
> When we had past the open portal thro', —
>   A rusty gate, because the greed of men
>   Maketh to them the crooked way look true, —
> My hearing told me it was closed again;
>   And if I had allowed mine eyes to turn,
>   Whatever could my fault have mended then?

Through Purgatory, Dante mounts to Heaven, and there, in the starry sphere, he undergoes an examination in the three Christian virtues by their

accepted representatives, St. Peter, St. James, and
St. John, who question him respectively on Faith,
Hope, and Love. Behold him, introduced by his
guide, in the presence of St. Peter, who appears
only as a great light. "Even as the candidate,
before the master puts the question, prepares his
defense in silence (to debate the problem, not to
decide it), so, while Beatrice was speaking, I was
equipping myself with every argument, to be ready
for so great an examiner and so great a profession. 'Speak, good Christian! declare thyself!
What is faith?' At that I lifted my brow toward
the light whence these words were breathed. Then
I turned to Beatrice, who quickly signaled to me
that I should pour forth the water of my soul's
fountain. 'May that grace,' I began, 'which
grants me the privilege of confessing to the high
commander, lend clear expression to my ideas!'
Then I continued: 'O father, as hath been written for us by the truthful pen of thy dear brother,
who, with thee, brought Rome into the line of
righteousness, faith is the substance of things
hoped for and the evidence of things not seen.
This seemeth to me to be its essence.' Thereupon
I heard: 'Right is thy thought, if thou under-
standest well why he [St. Paul] classed faith first
among substances, then among evidences.' And
I followed with my answer: 'The deep things
which I am here allowed to behold are so hidden
from men's eyes on earth that their existence,
down below, abides in belief alone, whereof our
profound hope is built; and therefore it falleth

into the category of substance. Moreover, from this same belief men are compelled to argue, without other proof; and therefore it belongeth to the class of evidences.' Then I heard: 'If all that is learned as doctrine, down on earth, were so clearly understood, there would be no place for the cunning of the sophist.' This was breathed from that flaming love, which then added: 'Already have the fineness and the weight of this coin been inspected carefully enough; but tell me whether thou hast it in thy purse.' And I replied: 'Yes, I have it, so round and bright that nothing in its stamp is obscure to me.' From the deep light that was glowing there, issued next these words: 'This precious jewel, foundation of all virtues, whence came it to thee?' 'The broad shower of the Holy Ghost,' said I, 'which is spread on the old parchments and the new, is a syllogism which hath proved it to me so sharply that, in comparison, every other demonstration appeareth dull to me.' 'The old and the new premise,' I then heard, 'which lead thee to this conclusion, why dost thou accept them as the word of God?' 'The proof that reveals the truth to me,' said I, 'is in the works performed [the miracles], for which nature never heated iron or struck anvil.' 'Speak!' was the answer: 'what warrant hast thou that these works really occurred? Thine only pledge is the very writ which is to be tested.' 'If the world,' I said, 'turned to Christianity without miracles, this one marvel is so great that all the others are but the hundredth part. For

thou didst come poor and hungry into the field to
sow that plant of righteousness, which once was
a vine but now is turned to a briar.'

"When this was ended, that holy court on high
reëchoed through the circles with *Te Deum lauda-
mus,* to the tune that is sung up yonder. And that
chief who already, in his examination, had drawn
me from branch to branch [of doctrine] so far
that we were now close to the topmost leaves [of
the tree], began once more: 'The grace that
fondles thy mind hath opened thus far thy lips as
they should be opened, wherefore I approve of
that which hath come forth; but now it behooves
thee to state what thou believest, and whence it
came to thy belief.' 'O holy father,' I began,
'O spirit who now beholdest that which once thou
didst believe so firmly as to outstrip the younger
feet into the sepulcher, thou wouldst have me
declare the essence of my unhesitating belief, and
thou hast asked also for the cause of it. Now this
is my reply: I believe in one God, single and eternal, who, unmoved himself, moveth all the heavens
with love and with longing. And for such belief
I not only have proofs physical and metaphysical,
but I receive it also from the truth that hath
been showered down from Heaven by Moses, by
prophets and psalms, by the Gospels, and by you
[Apostles] who did write, after the glowing spirit
made you holy. And I believe in three eternal
Persons; and these I believe to be an entity so one
and yet so threefold that it admits of a construction with *are* or *is*. The mysterious divine nature

[13]

whereof I now speak is stamped upon my mind more than once by the teaching of the Evangel. This is the beginning; this is the spark that presently swells into a lusty flame, and sparkles in me like a star in the sky.' "

> E'en as a lord, receiving joyous word,
> Thanketh the bearer, to his bosom prest,
> As soon as he the messenger hath heard,
> Thus me the saint melodiously blest,
> Three times encircling me, when I was done —
> That apostolic light, at whose behest
> I told my creed, which such approval won.

This curious passage (the last few lines of which I have tried to translate into verse) likens Dante's colloquy with St. Peter in the skies to an examination for the doctor's degree, the candidate being catechized by the professor. The subsequent tests in hope, administered by St. James, and in love, conducted by St. John, are less formal and less severe. Allegorically, Dante conceives of himself as being at this stage of his experience qualified for the highest flight of religious contemplation — for entrance into the realm of pure spirit, above the stars — by his proficiency in the three essential virtues of Christianity, which, no doubt, he now grasps with firmer certainty than ever before.

In his literal conception of Paradise, Dante thought of *certainty* as constituting one of its eternal joys. Those doctrines which on earth are received as a matter of faith, beyond our thorough comprehension, those mysteries which are far out of the reach of mortal penetration, shall in Heaven be as clear as any axiom, as the simplest geometrical proposition, as the plainest object our eyes behold. Those problems which so torment us by constantly whetting our intellectual curiosity shall be solved for us; our thirst for knowledge shall be satisfied.

During the poet's mystic progress through the heavens he continually receives from Beatrice, and from the other spirits he encounters, instruction in the abstruse problems of philosophy, ethics, and theology. These fictitious discussions, which, as I have said, often enough seem uninteresting to the modern reader, were surely a delight to their author as he invented them. To him they must have been as a foretaste of the real life after death. Among other things, he learns why it is that all the souls in Paradise are perfectly contented, although they do not all enjoy the same degree of blessedness : it is because each is blest to its utmost capacity for beatitude, and also because the greatest happiness for every one is the consciousness of conformity to the maker's intent. He is taught that injustice in God's decrees is not only impossible, but a downright contradiction of terms; for what we call justice is only another name for the divine will.

> Now wilt thou sit upon the bench, O man,
> To judge of things a thousand miles away
> With eyes that cannot see beyond a span?

But (we may ask, in our presumption) how can it be just that a virtuous pagan, who has never

heard of Christ, should be damned for not being
a Christian?

A man, thou sayst, is born on Indus' strand
  And none there is the tale of Christ to read
  Nor write nor preach abroad, in all the land.
Upright is he in every wish and deed
  And, in so far as human wit can tell,
  A sinless life in act and word doth lead.
He dieth unbaptized, an infidel.
  If he believe not, how is he to blame?
  What kind of justice sendeth him to Hell?

The answer is this: although Heaven cannot
be won without faith in Christ, such faith may be
miraculously inspired in a worthy pagan by divine
grace. And Dante invents as an example the
salvation of the Trojan prince Ripheus, an obscure character in Virgil's *Æneid,* described as
the most just and scrupulous of his countrymen.
That soul, the poet is told, "moved by grace
which flows from so deep a font that no created
sight ever fathomed it to the bottom, bent all its
love, here below, on justice; wherefore, proceeding from grace to grace, God opened its eyes to
our future redemption. And the soul believed
therein, and after that no longer could endure
the stench of paganism, but rebuked his people
for their perversity." The three Christian virtues
were his baptism, more than a thousand years
before men were baptized. "O predestination,"
cry the heavenly spirits that have expounded this
truth to Dante, "O predestination, how distant is
thy root from those minds which see not the
primal cause entire! Ye mortals, hold your judg-

ments in reserve; for we, who see God, do not yet know all the elect."

Predestination is a problem that never can be completely solved, even in Paradise. The mind of God, more profound than any created intelligence, can be fully understood only by itself. To the purest of the blest, even to the highest of the angels, the divine purpose is only partially apparent. But this ignorance does not disturb their bliss; for what God wills, they will. One thing, then, Dante can never hope to comprehend — the secret of the plan of salvation. Why has the Lord made one vessel unto honor, another unto dishonor? How can God's foresight and omnipotence be reconciled with man's absolute freedom and responsibility? For the individual human will is free: it has the choice between good and evil, it has conscience to guide it, it has opportunity to achieve salvation. If it fails, the fault is its own. How this can be, in spite of the foreknowledge of its maker, is a mystery that quite transcends the created mind.

By "predestination" Dante means, not the foredooming of certain souls to Hell, but the endowment of all souls, as they are made by God at the moment of the birth of the body, with distinct and different degrees of spiritual vision. All have sight enough to steer their course, if they make the best of what they have; but some see better than others. Now, if the soul, by its own effort, gains admission to Paradise, the kind of happiness it is destined to enjoy depends upon the clearness of

this sight. Heavenly spirits all see God, but they
see him diversely; and their beatitude is accord-
ingly diverse. " In my Father's house are many
mansions." Joy results from intensity of love,
and that results from intensity of vision, a prod-
uct of grace. This doctrine of predestination is
the dominant note of the *Paradiso,* as free will
is the leading theme of the *Purgatorio.* Dante
goes so far as to apply it even to babes that die
before exercising their will. In his Heaven their
seats are graded at different elevations — a symbol of different grades of blessedness — according
to the primal sight bestowed on them.

The mysteries that are to become clear as day,
as soon as we shall be released from the flesh, are
of a different nature, in that they do not involve
a sounding of the mind of God. When Dante
declared to St. Peter the substance of his creed,
you observed that it consisted of only two articles:
" I believe in one God, single and eternal, who,
unmoved himself, moveth all the heavens . . .
And I believe in three eternal Persons; and these
I believe to be an entity so one and yet so threefold that it admits of a construction with *are* or
is." The first doctrine, then, is that of the unity
and the universality of God, the one primal power
of the universe, unchanging and eternal. That
the Creator can remain indivisible and at the same
time contain all things, appears to the mortal
understanding an irreconcilable contradiction; but
to the eye of the spirit there is no inconsistency.
When the poet's heavenly journey culminates in

the direct vision of God, the divine nature is revealed to him, although afterwards he can remember nothing save that for one instant he understood. "O Grace abounding, which gave me
courage to pierce with my eyes the eternal splendor
until my mortal sight was quenched! Contained
within its depths I saw, bound by love into a single
volume, all that is scattered through the pages of
the universe, substance and accident and their
operation, so fused together, as it were, that the
thing whereof I speak is one simple light. I believe I *did* behold the universal principle of this
union, because, as I speak these words, I feel an
ampler sense of satisfaction." Another apparent
contradiction is involved in the second clause, the
doctrine of the Trinity, the three in one, which
Dante pictures as three circles of three different
colors but occupying exactly the same space.

In these two articles is carried implicitly all the
rest of Christian dogma: creation, original sin,
redemption. And the doctrine of redemption implies a third mystery beyond earthly — but not
heavenly — understanding, the union of two natures in the Redeemer. In Dante's Garden of
Eden, Christ is portrayed allegorically as a griffin,
which is one single creature composed of an eagle
and a lion: the eagle, monarch of the air, represents the divine nature; the lion, king of beasts,
the human. Each is perfectly distinct, yet the
two form but one. Within the glowing orb of
day many souls, brighter than the sun itself, are
singing together, as the ancients used to sing their

songs of praise to Bacchus and Apollo. But there, says Dante, " the chant was not of Bacchus, no Pæan was it, but a song of three Persons in the divine nature, and of the divine and the human nature in one Person." Again the same souls lift up their voices: " That One and Two and Three which liveth forever and forever reigneth in Three and Two and One, not circumscribed but circumscribing all, was thrice sung by each of those spirits with a melody that would be a sufficient reward for any merit." Let us go back to the beginning of the poet's celestial journey. Accompanied by Beatrice, he quits the earth, and, darting into the skies, penetrates the moon. Like St. Paul, he is not sure whether he has left his flesh behind: " whether in the body, or out of the body, I cannot tell: God knoweth." " Within itself," declares Dante, " the eternal pearl [the moon] received us, as water takes in a ray of sunlight, remaining unbroken. If I was in the flesh (and in this case it cannot be conceived how one solid admitted another, as must occur, if body enters into body) — if I was in the flesh, our eagerness should be all the hotter to behold that essence in which is to be seen the union of our nature with God. In it we shall *see* that which we hold by faith; it shall not be proved, but shall be self-revealed, even as the primal truth that all men believe."

The Creation was the materialization, the externalization, so to speak, of the universe which had existed from all eternity in the divine consciousness. The conception had always been

there. " In the beginning was the Word, and the
Word was with God, and the Word was God."
The *act* was performed by the three Persons of
the Trinity in unison: Power, moved by Love,
guided by Wisdom, made the wondrous world.
As Dante puts it: "All that revolves in space or
in mind was created, — with a symmetry such
that he who contemplates it cannot be without
some foretaste of its maker, — by the primal and
ineffable Power, gazing upon his Son with that
love which breathes eternally from each." It was
the divine bounty, the desire of God to share his
happiness with other beings, which impelled him
to bring into existence the angels and mankind
(endowed with free will, that they might have a
real life of their own), and to fashion the world
for them to inhabit — earth for man, skies for the
angels. "The divine goodness," says the poet,
" to which all envy is alien, glowing within itself,
sparkles so that it unfolds its eternal beauties."
A lovely image of creation: God's burning love
throwing off sparks, which repeat and multiply
its eternal light. In another passage Beatrice
expounds to Dante the motive of the creative act,
when, as we read in Genesis, " the Spirit of God
moved upon the face of the waters." " Not for
the sake of increasing his own welfare," she says,
" for that cannot be, but to the end that his brightness, reflected back, might say ' I live,' the eternal
love, at its own pleasure, in its eternity outside
of time and outside of every other restriction,
opened out into new loves. Nor did it lie, before

this act, in a state, as it were, of torpor; for there was no before nor after in the moving of God upon these waters." God, in his eternity, knows no distinctions of time, all moments being equally present to him. He is sometimes likened to the centre of a circle whose circumference is eternity; for the centre is simultaneously opposite all points of the circumference. As to the mode of creation, the Biblical six days are to be taken figuratively. The angels, the heavens, and the mass of brute matter burst into existence in one moment; then the skies, directed by the angels, operated upon matter, separating the four elements (earth, water, air, fire), shaping our globe, and drawing forth minerals, plants, and beasts; but man was created by a special, direct act of God.

Angels and men were created free; but freedom implies the possibility of sin. If there be no opportunity to make a wrongful choice, there can be no free will, and therefore no independent life. Beasts and plants can do no evil, for they are governed in all things by instinct, over which they have no control. Angels and men, destined to be participants in God's happiness, must be independent and must prove themselves worthy of their freedom. At the very outset of their career they are put to the test. The angels are offered grace, which most of them unhesitatingly accept, and forevermore, in consequence of this gift, behold God so clearly that it is impossible for them to deviate from his will. But some ("about a tenth," as Dante conjectures), expecting in their arrogance to equal God without his help, reject the proffered grace — "before one could count twenty " — and are cast out of Heaven to dwell everlastingly as devils in Hell, which shapes itself in the forming earth as they fall. Thereupon, to fill their vacant place, God created man. Adam and Eve were set in the Earthly Paradise, the intended home of humanity; they were surrounded with all the charms of perpetual springtime, and all their wants were supplied. Only one restriction was put upon them, and that they presently broke, exalting themselves, in their pride, above the divine law. Ere they were seven hours old, they were driven from Eden, and mankind had forfeited the gift of grace, had incurred the penalty of death, and had lost the way to Heaven. " Unwilling," says Dante, "to suffer any check upon his will power, — even a check to his own advantage, — that man who never was born, condemning himself, condemned all his progeny." In the trial of free will, the greater part of the angels had met their responsibility with success; humanity, in the person of our first father, potentially the wisest of men, had failed.

Yet divine love found a way for man's possible redemption. When Dante is in the sky which bears the fixed stars, he beholds, in the form of innumerable lights, the whole host of the human souls redeemed by Christ; and the Saviour himself shines forth like a fiery sun above them. " There was but a little while," writes the poet, " between one instant and the other: I mean, between my expecting and my beholding the sky grow brighter and ever brighter. And Beatrice cried: ' Lo! the armies of the triumph of Christ, and all the harvest gathered by the revolution of these spheres!' It seemed to me that her face was all afire, and her eyes so full of gladness that I must pass on without words. As, on clear, calm nights of full moon, Luna laughs among her eternal nymphs, who paint the sky on all sides, I saw shining, above thousands of lights, one sun which kindled them all, as our sun kindles the things we see on high; and through its living glow there shone the gleaming *substance* so clear that my sight could not support it." This " substance," which gleams through the splendor of Christ, is, of course, the human nature in his Person. In Dante's final vision of God, the second of the three rings of light appears to him to be " painted by itself, with its own color, in our likeness. Therefore was my attention all bent upon it. Like some geometer who applies his whole mind to the problem of squaring the circle, and in his thought cannot discover the principle he lacks, so was I before this strange sight. I was eager to see how the image was related to the circle, and what was its place therein; " but my wings could not soar so high — until in one instant, like a lightning-flash, my " wish came."

In spite of the divine assumption of man's nature with man's inherited sin, in spite of vicarious atonement, the salvation or perdition of each soul depends upon that soul itself. And it

depends specifically on the real state of the soul
at the very moment of death. This doctrine is
brought home to the reader of the *Divine Comedy*
by two contrary examples, one in Hell, one in
Purgatory, the two contrasted sinners being father
and son, Guido and Buonconte da Montefeltro.
In each case there is at death a contest, between
the powers of good and of evil, for the possession
of the soul, the demon winning in the first instance,
the angel in the second. The father, Guido, having made his peace with Heaven, commits one last
fault at the instigation of the Pope, Boniface VIII,
who promises to remit his guilt; he is lost. Buonconte, the son, at the close of an irreligious life,
being mortally wounded on the battle-field, calls
on Mary with his last gasp, and is saved. The
first has died unrepentant, though absolved by the
Pope; the second has died genuinely repentant,
though too late for earthly shriving.

Guido da Montefeltro was a great Ghibelline
general, renowned for his astuteness. His spirit
is found by Dante in Hell, among the fraudulent
counselors, enveloped and hidden by a huge tongue
of flame, which, moving its point, speaks the words
uttered by the soul within it. "When the fire,"
says the poet, "had roared a bit after its fashion,
it waved its sharp tip to and fro, and then gave the
following blast: ' If I believed that my reply were
made to one who was ever to return to the world,
this flame would shake no more. But since, if
what I hear is true, no one has ever gone back
alive from this depth, I answer thee without fear

of infamy. I was a man of arms, and then a
Franciscan, thinking to make amends by wearing
the rope girdle. And my thought would have
turned out true, had it not been for the high priest
(a curse upon him!), who led me back into my
former sins. And I would have thee hear how
and why. While I was a shape of bones and flesh,
which my mother gave me, my deeds were not
those of a lion but of a fox. Wiles and secret
ways, I knew them all, and so plied their art that
the fame of it went forth to the ends of the earth.
When I saw that I had reached that part of my
age when every man should furl his sails and coil
his ropes, I was grieved at the things that had
pleased me before. Penitent and confessed, I
took vows (poor me!); and it might have saved
me. The prince of the modern Pharisees, having
war close to the Lateran [with the Colonna
family] . . . , considered not his supreme office
and holy orders nor my rope belt . . . ; but, even
as Constantine sought Sylvester in Soracte to cure
his leprosy, so he sought me as a master-physician
to cure his haughty fever. He asked my advice,
and I was silent, because his words seemed to me
drunken. Then he spake: 'Let thy heart have no
misgiving. I absolve thee even now. And do
thou show me how I may bring to earth [the for-
tress of] Palestrina. I can lock and unlock
Heaven, as thou knowest, for I have the two
keys. . . .' At last his weighty arguments pushed
me to a point where silence appeared to me the
worse course, and I replied: 'Father, since thou

washest me clean of that sin into which I am about
to fall, a long promise and a short fulfilment shall
make thee triumph on thy high throne.' Then,
when I was dead, St. Francis came for me. But
one of the black Cherubim said to him: 'Take
him not, do not wrong me! He must come down
below among my servitors, because he gave that
counsel of fraud, ever since which I have been
lurking about his hair. For he who repents not
cannot be absolved, nor can anyone at the same
time repent and will [evil], because of the contradiction that will not admit of it.' Ah! woe is
me! How I shuddered when he seized me, saying: 'Perhaps thou didst not think that I had
studied logic!'"

Guido's son, Buonconte da Montefeltro, was,
like his father, an able captain. He was of our
poet's own time, and, in fact, was killed in 1289
at the battle of Campaldino in which Dante
fought, on the other side. Somehow his body
vanished from the field, and no one ever knew
what became of it. This mysterious disappear-
ance affords an opening for a story, which our
author puts into the mouth of Buonconte himself.
His shade is waiting on the mountain slope, outside
the gate of Purgatory, among those who, having
postponed repentance until the last moment, are
obliged to postpone correspondingly the entrance
upon their preparation for Heaven. Their delay
may, however, be shortened by the prayers of the
living. "'Prithee,'" he exclaimed to Dante, "'so
may *thy* longing be fulfilled which leads thee up

the high mountain, assist *my* longing with kindly piety. I was of Montefeltro; I am Buonconte. Neither Joan [my wife] nor anyone else takes thought of me; wherefore I walk among these [souls] with bended brow.' And I responded: 'What power or what chance so removed thee from Campaldino that thy burial place hath never been found?' 'O!' he replied, ' at the foot of the Casentino pours a stream named Archiano, which is born in the Apennines above the Hermitage. To the spot where its appellation becomes useless [because the river there merges with the Arno] I came, with my throat cut, fleeing on foot and wetting the plain with blood. There my sight failed, and my speech fled, ending with the name of Mary; and there I fell, and my flesh was left alone. I shall tell thee the truth, and do thou repeat it among the living. God's angel took me; and one from Hell shouted: "O thou from Heaven, why dost thou rob me? Thou shalt carry away this man's eternal part, all on account of one little tear, which snatches him from me. But of the rest I shall make a different disposal." Well thou knowest how the air collects that moist vapor which turns back to water as soon as it rises high enough to be caught by the cold. That spirit, combining intelligence with ill-will which seeks naught but harm, moved mist and wind with the power its nature gave it. Then, when the day was spent, it covered with clouds the valley between Pratomagno and the great chain, and made the sky above it so tense that the teeming air turned to water. The rain descended; and as much of it as earth could not support ran into gullies; and, coming together in great torrents, it plunged toward the royal river so swift that naught could check it. The raging Archiano found my frozen body at its mouth, and pushed it into the Arno, and undid upon my breast the cross that I had made of myself, when pain conquered me; it whirled me along banks and bottom, then swathed and begirt me with its booty.' "

Captain of his soul is every living Christian: his eternal fate depends eventually on himself. But man can find his Paradise only through Christ. " Neither is there salvation in any other: for there is none other name under heaven given among men, whereby we must be saved." The doctrines of his faith Dante accepted unreservedly, dwelt with them night and day, and, as we have seen, invested them in his mind with fresh substance and color. Unflinching belief in the power and goodness of God and the final triumph of justice, reverence for the external Church as the divinely established representative of the Church spiritual, close obedience to the rightful authority in matters of religion — all this was for him beyond question. Dante furiously resented the outrage done at Anagni to Pope Boniface VIII, whom he regarded, nevertheless, as an unscrupulous villain, doomed to Hell, the arch-enemy of his cause. Even the Emperor, whose independence Dante so passionately championed, must, according to him, respect the Pope as an elder son respects a father. The office, the religious function, was never confused by our poet with the man who exercised it. Unsparing he always was in criticism of the unworthy incumbent, untiring in his denunciation of wicked prelates; strict, too, in drawing the line between ecclesiastical dominion and individual right. A fraudulent absolution, as we have seen, is of no avail; equally impotent is an unjust excommunication. At the foot of the mountain of Purgatory Dante meets the shade of the beloved Manfred, chief of the Ghibellines, son of Emperor Frederick II. He, like his father, died under the ban of the Church. It was in 1266, at the great battle of Benevento, that he fell. His body was covered by his soldiers with a pile of stones, near the end of a bridge; but Pope Clement IV, unwilling to let his bones rest in peace, dispatched to the battle-field the Cardinal Archbishop of Cosenza, who had the remains disinterred and cast out of the papal realm, beside the river Verde. Yet Manfred, genuinely repentant at the end, — as Dante thought, — and a good Christian at heart, found forgiveness; whereas his father, the great Emperor, an impenitent heretic, was damned. I shall conclude with Manfred's story. Dante has been looking at a group of shades.

> And one began: " Whoe'er thou art, abide,
>   O thou that walkest on, look back again!
>   Hast ever seen me on the other side?
> I turned to him, and gazed with might and main.
>   Handsome and blond was he, a princely guest;
>   An ugly wound had cleft his brow in twain.

FAITH

When I with proper meekness had confest
  I ne'er had seen him, he exclaimed: " Now see! "
And showed a scar high up upon his breast.
" Manfred am I," he then said smilingly,
  " Grandson of Empress Constance, Henry's wife.
  And when thou shalt return, I beg of thee,
Seek out my beauteous daughter, who gave life
  To Aragon's and Sicily's great lords;
  Tell her the truth, if false report is rife.
When I was split by two death-dealing swords,
  My rueful soul I weeping did resign
  To him who gladly pardons and rewards.
My sins were horrible; but grace divine,
  With loving, all-embracing arms outspread,
  Takes every soul that doth to it incline.
And if Cosenza's shepherd, who was sped
  By Clement on my track, revenge to reap,
  That page of holy writ had rightly read,
My body's bones still peacefully would sleep
  Near Benevento, where the bridge is past,
  Protected by the ponderous stony heap.
Rain wets them now, and rattles them the blast,
  Outside the realm, not far from Verde's cleft,
  Where he, with lightless candles, had them cast.
No curse of theirs can leave us so bereft
  That God's eternal love may not come back,
  As long as hope hath any greenness left."

[From *Dante,* p. 41.]

LECTURE II

MORALITY

THE doctrine of free will, which I discussed in my first lecture, implies individual moral responsibility — a salutary principle, even though it be not in accord with the theories of sociology or the inclinations of sentiment. Nowadays we are all too disposed to put the blame for wrongdoing on heredity, environment, organization — anywhere but on the wrongdoer. However beautiful the impulse that prompts to such extenuation of crime, it certainly does not tend to check criminality. Dante's age knew no such amiable weakness. The criminal was not yet encouraged to look upon himself as a victim, rather than an offender, and consequently knew what to expect, here and hereafter. And Dante himself admitted no compromise with sin: a stern judge both of other men's deeds and of his own, he held all to the strictest account.

Sin is a wicked act of the will; and it consists in an erroneous choice between good and evil, the latter seeming under the circumstances preferable to the former. If we are attracted by unworthy things, it is not our fault: sin begins when we give way to the attraction, against the advice of conscience. Temptation is man's lot. Without it,

[32]

indeed, he would have no active free will, because there would be no choice to make. Temptation and heavenly protection are prettily figured in a scene in the *Purgatorio*. A company of spirits in a valley on the mountainside, below the gate of Purgatory, as night draws near, sing the Ambrosian hymn *Te lucis ante terminum*:

> Ere daylight wholly vanisheth,
> Creator, thee we supplicate
> That in thine endless clemency
> Thou guard us and watch over us.
>
> Let dreams be far away from us,
> Nocturnal phantoms flee from us;
> And hold in check our enemy,
> Lest he defile our purity.

[From Dante, p. 93.]

Here is the incident, as Dante tells it. " It was already the hour which inclines the longing of sailors and melts their hearts on the day they have said farewell to their dear friends, and which pricks with love the unaccustomed traveler if he hears from afar a bell that seems to mourn the dying day, when I began to gaze [with all the power of my senses] on one of the souls which had arisen and with its hand was asking for attention. It clasped and lifted up both palms, fixing its eyes on the east, as if saying to God, ' I care for naught else.' *Te lucis ante* issued so devoutly from its lips, and with such sweet notes, that it made me forget myself. And the other souls then sweetly and devoutly accompanied it through the whole

hymn, their eyes bent on the heavenly wheels.
Sharpen thine eyes here, reader, for the truth; for
now is the veil indeed so thin that surely it is easy
to see through. I beheld that gentle host then
silently look upward, as if waiting, pale and meek;
and I saw, issuing from on high and descending,
two angels with two fiery swords, blunted and
pointless. Green as little new-born leaves were
their garments, which trailed after them flapped
and fanned by green wings. The one took its
station a little above us, and the other alighted
on the opposite bank, so that the company within
[the valley] was between them. Well I saw their
blond heads, but their faces dazzled my eye, as
any excess benumbs a faculty. 'They both come
from the lap of Mary,' said Sordello, 'to watch
over the dell, because of the serpent that is coming
presently.' At that, I, not knowing in which direction, turned around, and, all chilly, drew close to
the trusty shoulders [of my leader]."

The two green angels of hope, with their
swords of defense, have come to guard these waiting souls against the serpent of temptation. After
some converse in the valley, the episode continues:
"While Virgil was speaking, Sordello drew the
speaker to himself, saying: 'Behold yonder our
enemy!' and pointed his finger to make Virgil
look that way. On the side where the little dale
has no bank, there was a snake, perhaps the one
that gave Eve the bitter food. Amid grass and
flowers I could see its evil trail advancing; and
from time to time it turned its head to its back,

licking like a creature that is sleeking itself. How
the heavenly hawks started I did not see and therefore cannot tell, but I clearly saw them both in
motion. Hearing the air cleft by the green
wings, the serpent fled, and the angels faced
about, flying evenly back to their posts."

The *Purgatorio* offers us another picture of
temptation — the dream of the Siren, who represents the sins of the flesh. Just before dawn
there appears to Dante in his sleep a hideous
female, misshapen, pallid, squint-eyed, stammer-
ing. "I gazed at her; and as the sun restores the
cold limbs made heavy by night, thus my look
loosened her tongue, then straightened her all out
in a little while, and colored her wan face as love
demands. When her speech was thus unbound,
she began to sing so that I could hardly have
turned my attention from her. 'I am,' she sang,
'I am sweet Siren who bewitch sailors in mid sea,
so full am I of charm to hear. By my song I
turned Ulysses from his wandering way. And
whosoever abides with me seldom departs, so
wholly do I satisfy him.' Her lips were not yet
closed when a lady, swift and holy, appeared at
my side, to confound the other. 'O Virgil, Virgil,
who is this?' she said proudly; and he advanced
with his eyes fixed only on this modest woman."
Virgil, or Reason, thus invoked by conscience
("the power that counsels") seizes the Siren,
which has come to look beautiful under Dante's
too attentive gaze, and reveals its true ugliness;
and Dante wakes from his dream in disgust.

Still another allegory of sin presents itself at the very beginning of the *Divine Comedy*. The poet, as you remember, suddenly comes to his senses in the early morning of good Friday, and finds himself in a dark wood, in which he has been wandering by the light of the full moon. Terrified and eager to escape, he makes his way to the foot of a mountain, whose summit is lit by the rays of the rising sun. But as he is attempting to climb this peak of righteousness, his evil habits, in the form of three beasts, bar his way and are on the point of driving him back into the wood of worldliness. Then it is that Reason, embodied in Virgil, appears on the scene, having been sent by Revelation, or Beatrice, at the instance of Grace and Mercy.

> " A very different way thy steps must trace,"
> Virgil replied, when he beheld me weep,
> " If thou wouldst leave this wild and woody place."

It is impossible to hurry thus from wickedness to rectitude, prompted only by fear. To escape from sin, one must know what sin really is, by contemplating it in its true light, by tracking it to its lair and seeing it in all its ugliness and folly; then, when evil has become abhorrent, — hateful in itself, not merely in its consequences, — one must submit to long, hard discipline, making amends for past wrong and fortifying the soul against future temptation. In a word, one must pass through Hell and Purgatory. " Wherefore," says Virgil, " for thine own good I judge and choose that thou follow me, and I shall be thy guide; and I shall lead thee where thou shalt hear the shrieks of despair and shalt see the ancient spirits in their pain, each one of them proclaiming the second death. Then thou shalt see those who are contented in the fire, because they expect, whenever the time may be, to come among the blest." In Dante's Hell, every punishment is the symbolic presentment of a sin; and the whole *Inferno* is an image of the wicked life of the depraved. In his Purgatory, the penalties represent the kinds of discipline required to cleanse the soul of its tendency to do wrong; and the *Purgatorio* is a picture of the penitent. One must learn the true nature of sin, and how to cure its effects. " ' O poet,' " Dante answers, " ' I implore thee by that God whom thou knewest not — that I may escape this ill and worse — to lead me whither thou hast just said, so that I may see St. Peter's gate and also those whom thou dost picture in such agony.' Then he set forth, and I followed after him."

Frank recognition of evil is Dante's course, not cowardly hiding or prevarication; resolute self-discipline, not shifting of responsibility or reliance on mercy. And when the path of reformation has once been chosen, there must be no delay, no diversion, no waste of time or strength. Virgil, himself devoid of hope of salvation, thus addresses a band of spirits who have started on the way to Heaven:

"O happily departed souls elect,
   I beg you, by the peace," said Virgil's ghost,
"Which I believe that all of you expect,

To tell us where to find a sloping coast,
    Inclined enough for man to climb the mount.
Wisest is he who values time the most."

The Ready-to-halt of the *Divine Comedy* is a
certain Belacqua, who in life had been a maker of
musical instruments and a friend of our poet in
Florence. The two travelers come across him on
the slant of the mountain, outside of Purgatory.
Virgil has been explaining the astronomy of the
southern hemisphere to Dante, who has observed
with amazement the sun taking its course across
the sky to the northward of the zenith instead of
to the southward. " 'If it is thy pleasure,' " says
the pupil, " 'I should like to know how far we
have to go; for the hillside rises higher than my
eyes can follow.' And the master replied: 'This
mountain is of such kind that it is always hard at
the base, when one begins; and the further up one
goes, the less it tires. Therefore, when it shall
seem to thee so gentle that the climb shall be as
easy for thee as going downstream in a boat, then
shalt thou be at the end of this path. There shalt
thou stop to rest thy heaving chest. I can give no
further answer, but this much I verily do know.'
Hardly had he finished his speech, when a voice
was heard close by: ' Perhaps, ere that, thou shalt
feel the need of sitting down.' At the sound,
each of us turned about, and we saw on our left
a great boulder, which neither he nor I had noticed
before. Thither we betook ourselves, and beheld
persons loitering in the shade, behind the rock,
like people who have thrown themselves down

in idleness. One of them, who had a weary look, sat clasping his knees, his face sunk low between them. 'O sweet my lord,' said I, 'look at that one, who appears lazier than if indolence had been his sister!' Then the spirit turned to us, and gave heed, lifting its face up only along the thigh, and said: 'Climb away, thou who art so speedy!' At that I recognized him; and the panting which still quickened my breath a little, did not prevent me from going to him. When I had reached him, he scarcely raised his head, saying: 'Hast thou really observed how the sun drives his chariot over thy left shoulder?' His sluggish ways and scanty words moved my lips to smile a little at first; then I began: 'Belacqua, now I am no longer anxious about thee. But tell me, why art thou sitting right here? Art thou waiting for an escort, or has thine old habit got thee again?' 'Brother,' he replied, 'what is the use of going up? The bird of God, who sits at the gate, would not admit me to the punishments.'"

An amused indulgence is Dante's feeling toward this good but drowsy soul. Even more sympathetic is his attitude toward those whom worldly but useful pursuits have for a while retarded on the road to self-perfection. Yet all of these, he warns us, have a score to pay: voluntary delay on earth shall be punished by involuntary delay on the ascent to blessedness. No dallying is safe. The sweetest, noblest of pleasures must not be allowed to interfere with our stern purpose. Such is the significance of the episode of Casella. This

Casella, another Florentine friend of Dante's, was
a composer, a little of whose music is preserved in
two Vatican manuscripts. We are perhaps not
over-bold in conjecturing that he wrote the melody
for some of our poet's songs. His soul is seen
on the shore of the island of Purgatory — an
island consisting mainly of a huge mountain, and
situated in the middle of the great ocean, opposite
Jerusalem. Thither, from the Tiber's mouth, an
angel ferries the departed souls that are on their
way to Paradise. A boat-load of these spirits has
just been landed, shortly after Dante and Virgil,
climbing out of Hell, have emerged on the same
strand.

" The newly arrived people raised their brows
toward us, and said: ' If ye know, show us the
way to go to the mountain.' And Virgil answered:
' Ye think, perhaps, that we are accustomed to
this place, but we are strangers, like you. We
came but a short while ago, a little before you, by
a different path, which was so rough and hard that
climbing will now seem to us like sport.' The
shades, which had now observed, from my breathing, that I was still alive, turned pale with wonder.
And, as a crowd hies to an olive-bearing messenger
to hear the news, and no one is afraid to tread
upon his neighbor's heels, so all those happy
souls fastened their eyes on my face, almost forgetting to go and make themselves beautiful.
One of them I saw coming forward to embrace
me, with such great affection that I was moved to
do the same. O shades empty, save to the eye!

MORALITY

Three times I clasped my hands behind it, and
three times I brought them back to my breast.
I think I must have taken on the color of amazement; for the shade smiled and drew back, and
I, pursuing it, pushed forward. Gently it bade me
desist. Then I recognized it, and besought it to
stay a little while to speak with me. It answered:
'Even as I loved thee when I was in the mortal
body, so I love thee now that I am set free; therefore I stop. But why journeyest thou?' 'Casella
mine,' said I, 'this way I am taking that I may
some time return to the place where I am now.
But why art thou robbed of so much time?' [Ca-
sella died some months ago, but his soul has just
arrived.] 'No wrong is done me,' he replied,
'if he who takes when and whom he chooseth,
hath more than once denied me this passage. For
his will is derived from a will that is just' . . .
Then I said: 'If no new law deprives thee of the
memory or the habit of lovely song, which used to
soothe all my desires, prithee, comfort a little my
soul therewith, which, bringing its body here, is
so weary.' Then he began *Amor che nella mente
mi ragiona* [one of Dante's own songs] so sweetly
that the sweetness still resounds within me. My
master and I and those who were with him seemed
as content as if not one of them had another
thought. We were all absorbed and intent on his
notes, when lo! the venerable elder [Cato, guard-
ian of the island, symbol of Free Will] appeared,
shouting: 'What is this, dilatory spirits? What
neglect, what dallying is this? Run to the moun-

[41]

tain to strip off the scales which prevent your eyes
from seeing God!'" Like frightened doves
startled at their repast, the new-come spirits flee
toward the mountainside, "as a man who goes,
not knowing whither." "Nor was *our* departure
less sudden." In this abrupt scattering, Dante
clings close to his trusty companion; "for how
could I have run without him? who would have
led me up the mountain?"

> Remorseful Virgil lookt, and pondering.
> O conscience clean and sure of good intent,
> How sharply thee a petty fault doth sting?

Weakness and irresolution were hateful to
Dante's positive, energetic nature. Theoretically,
to be sure, when no question of right or wrong is
involved, and two courses of the same attractive-
ness lie before us, hesitation is not only innocent
but inevitable. It is the old case of the donkey
between two bales of hay, or of "how happy could
I be with either." That was once the plight
of our poet, who, having two equally pressing
questions to ask, could not make up his mind which
to put: "Between two foods, one just as alluring
and just as distant as the other, a man with free
choice would die of hunger before he would set
his teeth in either. Thus a lamb would stand still
between two fierce, ravening wolves [afraid to
turn either way]. Thus a hound would stand
motionless between two deer. Wherefore, if
I was silent, pushed equally by my queries, I do
not blame nor praise myself, since it could not be
helped."

A different problem confronts a person who, having made a vow, finds the fulfilment of it disastrous. Here there *is* a question of right and wrong, however immediately harmful the right may appear. Of course, the only kind of a vow that enters into consideration is a proper one, a promise of such sort that God has received it — not a foolish pledge, like Jephthah's. To argue that one could, by breaking an accepted bond, accomplish something better than what has been plighted, is like purposing to dispense charity with stolen money. Nevertheless, the temptation may be very severe, and the wrong choice may look very justifiable. In Dante's Heaven, the lowest degree of beatitude is enjoyed by the souls of those who have been guilty of this weakness, but have won salvation by repentance. The figures he represents are those of nuns who, under compulsion from their families, have returned to secular life and married. They are seen as pale, faint images against the white moon — so dim that Dante at first takes them for reflections, making a mistake contrary to that of Narcissus, who fell in love with his own likeness in a fountain. "As the outlines of our features, in clean, transparent window panes, or in waters clear and still and not so deep that the bottom is invisible, return to us so feeble that a pearl against a white forehead is no slower in reaching our pupils, so I beheld several faces eager to speak. Wherefore I fell into an error opposite to that which kindled love between man and spring. No sooner had I taken note of them than I turned my eyes around, thinking these images to be mirrored forms, to see whose they might be. And, seeing nothing, I turned to the front again, looking toward the light of my dear guide, whose holy eyes were aglow with smiles."

These figures, feeble and indeterminate though they be, are not scornfully depicted. They are gentle, well-meaning creatures, who lack the clean-cut vigor of those men and women whose spiritual sight is clearest. On. earth they suffered sorely and patiently from their mistaken course, and in Paradise their happiness is of the mildest variety. How different is Dante's portrayal of the selfish Laodiceans, the time-serving neutrals, who, when the battle of righteousness was being fought, would take neither side, preferring the life and ease of the body to the life of the spirit! For such souls as these he provides a dwelling apart, within the gate of Hell, but outside the encircling river Acheron, a sort of vestibule of the lower world. Tormented beyond endurance by trifles (as are always those who put their own comfort above everything else), forever dodging purposelessly to and fro after a flag that leads to nothing, they suffer a punishment that is invested with no dignity and arouses no sympathy. Here is Dante's description.

" Now sighs, cries, and shrill shrieks rang through the starless air; whereat at first I began to weep. Strange tongues, horrid speech, words of pain, accents of wrath, voices loud and weak,

and the sound of hands accompanying them, made
a tumult which revolves forever in that air endlessly dark, like sand blowing before a whirlwind.
And I, whose head was hooded with horror, exclaimed: ' Master, what is it I hear? What kind
of people is it that seems so vanquished by grief?'
And he replied: 'This is the miserable way followed by the sorry souls of those who lived without infamy and without glory. They are mingled
with the mean choir of those angels who were not
rebels and were not faithful to God, but were for
themselves. Heaven cast them out, lest its beauty
should be spoiled; and deep Hell will not receive
them, because the damned might derive some satisfaction from them.' ' Master,' said I, ' what is
so grievous to them, which makes them complain
so loud?' 'I shall tell thee right briefly,' he
answered. ' These people have no hope of death,
and their blind life is so vile that they are envious
of any other lot. The world allows no report of
them to last; mercy and justice disdain them. Let
us not speak of them, but look and pass by!' And
I, looking, saw a banner, which ran circling so swift
that it seemed scornful of all rest; and after it
there came trailing such a long train of people that
I should never have thought death had undone so
many. When I had made out one or two of them,
I saw and recognized the shade of him who, for
cowardice, made the great refusal. Forthwith
I understood and was convinced that this was the
sect of poltroons, obnoxious both to God and to
God's enemies. These luckless creatures, who

never had been really alive, were naked and badly stung by flies and wasps which were there. These insects streaked their faces with blood, which, mixed with tears, was caught by disgusting worms at their feet."

Not one of these souls is named by the poet. One, and only one, is so described as to admit of possible identification — he " who, for cowardice, made the great refusal." This is in all probability Celestine V, Pope in 1294, a simple, pious man, inadequate to his great trust, who quickly abdicated, leaving the office to the hated Boniface VIII. An old legend relates that after his renunciation he fled from place to place, seeking to hide his shame: but wherever he went, he was recognized, pointed out, and called by name, even by those who had never seen him before.

So much for those who, instead of confronting evil manfully, try to avoid it. Dante, as we have just seen, has little mercy on them, although he apprehended, as clearly as anyone who ever lived, what a terrifying thing evil is. More and more its horror swells, as we follow the poet through the ranks of the damned, until the awfulness reaches its culmination in the gigantic figure of Satan, — monarch of Hell, embodiment of all wickedness, — planted for eternity in the centre of the earth, fixed in the middle of the round plain of ice, at the bottom of the pit, over which Virgil and Dante are traveling.

" ' The standards of the King approach — the king of Hell — drawing near to us. Therefore look ahead,' said my master, ' and see whether thou canst discern him.' As, when a thick fog is blowing, or when our hemisphere is wrapped in night, a mill looks from afar, if turned by the wind, such an engine I thought I saw then. But the wind made me cower behind my leader, for there was no other shelter. Already, and with fear I set it to metre, I was where the shades were wholly covered [by the ice], and showed through like a bit of straw in glass. Some are prostrate, others erect, others, like a bow, curve face to feet. When we had gone so far ahead that it was my master's pleasure to disclose to me the creature which once had the form of beauty, he stepped out from before me, saying: 'Lo! Dis, and lo! the place where thou must arm thyself with strength.' How cold and limp I then became, ask not, reader, for I write it not, because any speech would fall short. I did not die, nor did I remain alive: now consider for thyself, if thou hast a grain of wit, what I became, bereft of both. The emperor of the realm of grief projected from the ice from half-way up his chest; and I am more comparable to a giant than giants are to his arms. Now see how big the whole must be which is proportionate to such a part. If he was once as fair as he is ugly now, and [nevertheless] lifted his brows against his Maker, it is right indeed that all mourning should proceed from him. Oh! what a mighty marvel it seemed to me when I beheld three faces on his head! One was in front, and that was red; the other two joined this just above the middle of either shoulder, and met where the crest is. The right hand one looked between white and yellow; the left was such to see as come from the country where the Nile descends. Under each one jutted two huge wings, big as befitted such a great bird: I never saw ship's sails to match them. They had no feathers, but batlike was their style. These he flapped, so that three winds issued from him, by which all Cocytus was frozen. With six eyes he was weeping, and over three chins drooled tears and bloody slaver. With each mouth he was crushing a sinner between his teeth, like a heckle, so that three of them were tortured thus. For the one in front the biting was nothing, compared to the scratching, for now and again his spine would be all stripped of skin. 'That soul up yonder, which has the worst punishment,' said my master, 'is Judas Iscariot, who has his head within and brandishes his legs outside. Of the other two, whose heads are below, the one dangling from the black snout is Brutus — see how he writhes, without a word; and the other is Cassius, who looks so stout of limb. But night is rising up again, and now we must go; for we have seen all.'"

Such is sin, degenerate, hideous, fearful — three-faced, in opposition to the three Persons of the Holy Trinity. The three faces correspond, it would seem, to the three kinds of wickedness; so do the three winds, which symbolize diabolical suggestion. Dante's classification of wrongdoing is based on Aristotle, although his phraseology is

somewhat colored by Cicero. His Hell falls into
three parts, containing respectively faults of weakness, violence, and fraud. Aristotle's *weakness*
the poet calls "incontinence," or lack of self-
control; this category comprises luxury, gluttony,
avarice, prodigality, anger, which are placed in
the Upper Hell. In the Lower Hell, or City of
Dis, are the other two classes. *Violence,* which
is Cicero's term, corresponds in Dante's scheme
to Aristotle's "bestiality:" murder, robbery, sui-
cide, blasphemy of word or deed are sins of
violence, directed against one's fellow creatures,
one's self, or God. Cicero's *fraud* is equivalent to
Aristotle's "malice"; and Dante puts it at the
bottom of the list. It is subdivided, according as
the deception is practised on persons who have no
special reason for confidence, or on those who are
bound to the deceiver by a particular tie of kinship, patriotism, hospitality, or benefaction: on the
one hand we have cheats; on the other, traitors.
These last are the worst sinners of all — men with
hearts of ice and souls of fiends, who have perverted the gift of intelligence to an instrument of
pure evil. And worst among them are the three
we have just seen in the jaws of Lucifer: Judas,
who betrayed the founder of the Church; Brutus
and Cassius, who betrayed the founder of the
Empire. In this philosophical plan there is no
place for the specifically Christian sins of unbelief.
For virtuous pagans and unbaptized children the
Church had provided a *limbus,* or "fringe" of
the lower world: this limbus Dante locates at the

top of his Upper Hell; for heretics he invents a somewhat similar edge, or brink, at the top of his Lower Hell. Outside the frontier, but within the gate, as we have noted, is his vestibule for neutrals.

Dante's Hell is a vast cavern under the crust of our globe. Its general shape is conical, with the apex at the earth's centre. The lost souls and the demons inhabit terraces that encircle its declivity. Of course he had no idea that his elaboration of detail corresponded to the real facts: his topography is symbolic, illustrative of his classification of sins. But Hell as a whole, a place of eternal, horrible, merciless punishment, probably underground, was to him an absolute reality. In all probability, he believed also that this punishment is physical, that Hell-fire is to be taken literally, not metaphorically: at least, that is the conclusion reached by his master, St. Thomas Aquinas, who points out, however, that the paradox of disembodied spirits tortured by material means is beyond human comprehension. Endless and hopeless agony is the lot of those mortals, who, of their own free choice, in spite of God's sacrifice of himself, in spite of the offer of forgiveness up to the very moment of death, persist in their ungrateful rebellion against their Maker, and prove themselves unworthy to dwell with the blest. If the Lord's justice is as unrelenting as his mercy is untiring, if he can damn forever the unchangeably wicked, surely the just man, merciful though he be by nature, has reason to assume toward wickedness an attitude of uncompromising hate. The more we love God, the more we abhor his enemies.

Purgatory, likewise, was entirely real to our poet, more definitely fixed by tradition in its detailed arrangement, but more vaguely located as a whole. Dante, in his symbolic invention, happily places it, not in the gloomy inside of the earth, but, as we have seen, on the surface, around the upper slopes of a huge mountain that rises from an island in the middle of the sea. Running about the peak are seven narrow shelves, on which the souls of repentant sinners are doing penance for the sins for which atonement was not made before death. The terraces are seven because seven are the capital vices, the evil tendencies acquired by humanity, the sources of all varieties of sin. By making amends in Purgatory for their past misdeeds, the spirits are eradicating the inclination to wickedness, purifying themselves and preparing themselves for Heaven. This reformatory function of Purgatory is so stressed by Dante as almost to obscure its merely retributive purpose. The torments are, to be sure, terrible, and may last for centuries, but their duration is as nothing compared to an eternity of blessedness which is sure to ensue, and they are undertaken willingly, cheerfully by the penitents, even as we gladly accept a bitter medicine, knowing that it will restore our health. The burden of Dante's *Purgatorio* is the joy and hopefulness of self-discipline.

The seven fundamental vices, or evil human

habits, are, beginning with the worst: pride, envy, anger, sloth, avarice and prodigality, gluttony, luxury. Four of these have corresponding places in Dante's Hell. The other three — pride, envy, sloth — manifest themselves in various kinds of wrongdoing, which wicked acts form the basis of classification in the world of the damned. Pride, indeed, is at the bottom of all sin, and envy is responsible for many of the worst crimes. The penance of the proud is self-humiliation: crushed and crouching under heavy weights, which they carry on their backs, they crawl slowly and painfully around their terrace. The envious must practise self-denial: in the garb and posture of beggars, they sit on the ground, along the wall, their eyes closed by an iron wire which sews them up.

> I do not think there walks the earth to-day
> A man so hard as not to feel the stab
> Of sympathy for what before me lay.

Among the repentant proud is Provenzano Salvani, "who takes up so little of the way; once all Tuscany reëchoed with his name, and now it is barely whispered in Siena, which he ruled." His pride was the pride of power. His entrance to Purgatory was hastened by an act of humility performed on earth. One of his friends having been captured by Charles of Anjou and held for a high ransom, Provenzano, curbing his haughtiness, took his stand in the public square of Siena and begged of the passers-by until he had collected the amount. This self-mortification, which, the poet says, " made him to quiver in every vein," won him an advance in the other world. A second of the penitents represents pride of birth. Omberto Aldobrandesco, count of Santafiore, whom " his ancient blood and the fair deeds of his ancestors made so arrogant that, forgetting our common mother, he held every man in contempt." A third spirit is doing penance for the pride of art. " As I walked," says Dante, " I bent my face down, and one of them — not the one who had been speaking — twisted himself under the weight that bowed him, and saw and recognized me, and called to me, with difficulty keeping his eyes fixed on me, who walked all stooping like the rest. 'Oh!' said I to him, ' art thou not Oderisi, the glory of Gubbio, and the glory of that art which in Paris is termed *illuminating?*' ' Brother,' he answered, ' the pages that Franco Bolognese paints are more smiling than mine. The glory is now all his — and mine in part. Never should I have been so courteous while I was alive, because of my great craving to excel, on which my heart was set. Here I am paying the forfeit for that pride. And I should not yet be here, if it were not that, while I still had strength to sin, I turned to God. O vain glory of human power! What a little while the green lasts at the tip of the tree, unless ignorant generations follow! Cimabue once thought to hold the field in painting, and now Giotto has the cry, so that *his* fame is darkened. Thus one Guido hath robbed the other of the glory of the pen; and haply someone is already born who shall

[53]

drive them both from the nest. Earthly reputation is naught but a blast of wind, which blows now from this side, now from that, and changes its name when it changes its quarter.'" The two Guidos are Guido Guinizelli, Dante's predecessor and model, and Guido Cavalcanti, Dante's "first friend." Something of the pride of art — a most legitimate pride if any be lawful — our author had himself; for he knew of course that the "someone already born" would suggest to the reader the poet's own name and no other. Pride of birth he had also, as we shall see later. In fact, he seems to have regarded pride as his besetting sin. That is what he means, when he speaks of bending and stooping like the burdened spirits who are being punished for that sin, and when he continues: "side by side, like oxen under the yoke, I walked beside that laden soul."

Envy, on the other hand, is a sin to which Dante thought himself but little addicted. As he is passing by the row of blinded penitents on the terrace of the envious, he feels embarrassed at his own freedom from their torment. "It seemed to me that I was insulting them as I walked along, seeing others, but not seen by them; and I turned to my wise counselor. He well knew what my dumb show meant, and therefore did not await my question, but said: 'Speak, and be brief and to the point!' Virgil was beside me on that side of the shelf from which one might have fallen off, because it is encircled by no parapet. On the other side of me were the devout shades, whose tears so pressed through their horrible stitches that they wet their cheeks. I turned to them and spake: 'O company sure of beholding that heavenly light upon which alone your desire is bent, tell me — so may grace quickly melt the scum of your conscience and let the stream of memory run through it undefiled! — tell me (and it shall be dear and precious to me) whether any soul here among you is Italian; and perhaps it will be well for that spirit, if I am told.' 'O brother mine, each one of us is a citizen of a true city. But thou meanest one who lived in Italy during his pilgrimage.' This I seemed to hear as a reply a little further on than the place where I was standing; and so I made myself heard a bit ahead. Among the others I saw a shade that looked as if it were waiting; and if anyone should ask 'How [did it show it]?' [I should answer], it was lifting up its chin like a blind man. 'Spirit,' said I, 'that dost discipline thyself in order to ascend, if thou art the one that replied to me, reveal thyself by town or name.' 'I was from Siena,' it responded, 'and with these others I am here cleansing my guilty life, weeping to God, that he may lend himself to us. Prudent was I not, although my name was Prudence, and I took more pleasure in other people's disasters than in my own good luck. And to show thee that I am not deceiving thee, hear whether I was mad as I say, when I was already on the downward slant of my years. My fellow-citizens had come to battle with their enemies near Colle; and I was praying God for something that he had already decreed. There they were broken and turned to bitter flight; and seeing the rout I felt joy beyond any other — such joy that I lifted my bold face to Heaven, crying to the Lord: " Now I fear thee no more!" as the blackbird does when there is a little fair weather. Peace I sought with God at the end of my life; but my debt would not yet be lessened by penance, were it not that Peter the Comb-seller, who in his charity was sorry for me, remembered me in his holy prayers.' "

While the punishments in Purgatory are terrible, none of them are disgusting or grotesque, as are many of those in Hell. The penitents are on their way to Heaven, and therefore worthy of respect and sympathy, however hard their way may be. The damned, all of them, merit only hatred and contempt. However, the Dante who journeys through Hell is still a sinner, moved by human impulses; and this imperfection of the protagonist allows the poet freedom to manifest his own reaction to various kinds of wickedness. The sight of ferocious wrath excites him to such a pitch of indignation that he is eager to see the worst retribution wreaked on it. In the presence of treachery, he is impelled to do violence to the sinners himself, and even to cheat one of them cruelly by a false promise. Amorousness, on the contrary, makes him swoon with pity. By wrangling and strife he is fascinated, against his better judgment. The fate of soothsayers and sorcerers moves him to tears, for which he is sharply re-

buked by Virgil. Dante's own feeling toward the
different types of wrongdoing is shown not only
in the varying attitude he ascribes to himself in
the narrative (this is doubtless due in large measure to theoretical reasons) but also, and on the
whole more surely, in the nature of the penalties
he metes out to them. In the plan of his Hell
and his classification of sins there is nothing emotional, his arrangement being objectively philosophical. But in his assignment of punishments
we can see something of the author's individual
preferences and repugnances.

Some sins evidently aroused in Dante only
loathing. Most loathsome of all is flattery, which
is very briefly disposed of, in terms of untrans-
latable nastiness. Flattery the poor exile must
have learned to know and to hate, when he was
dependent on the hospitality of the rich, a com-
petitor — and doubtless a frequently unsuccessful
one — for their favor. Gluttony excited in him
nothing but disgust, although he might feel sympathy and affection for a glutton who had re-
deeming qualities. Forese Donati was his close
friend. To Ciacco, in Hell, the poet says: "Thy
anguish grieves me so that it bids me weep." The
torment itself, however, has in it nothing suggestive of tenderness. Gluttony is punished in
the Upper Hell in the third circle:

> Into the third, the ring of rain I came —
> Unending rain, accursed, heavy, cold,
> In kind and fall eternally the same.
> Thick hail and snow and water dark and old

> Pour ever down and down the murky air;
> And stinks the ground which all the stuff doth hold.
> Here fierce uncanny Cerberus hath his lair,
> Three-throated barketh, even as a dog,
> O'er all the people who are sunken there.

At the approach of the travelers, Cerberus, the embodiment of greediness, opens his maws and shows his fangs, quivering in every limb; but Virgil pacifies him by casting into his mouths a handful of mud.

> As barks a hungry dog, on eating bent,
> And then is silent when he bites his meat,
> On bolting it combatively intent,
> E'en so those filthy muzzles were replete.

Avarice was abhorrent to Dante, and he repeatedly inveighs against it as the vice most fatal to mankind. Yet his conscience told him that it was intrinsically no worse than prodigality, to which the poet himself — as we have reason to believe — was somewhat prone. Both are sins of excess, departures from moderation, in the use of money. Therefore, in Purgatory as in Hell, avarice and prodigality are classed together and subjected to the same retribution. In fact, in the lower world, Dante sets aside those mad spendthrifts who run to destruction, and places them far below the misers, on a level with the suicides. The essential feature of both ordinary stinginess and ordinary lavishness is, to Dante's mind, its laborious futility. Human beings, capable of the highest flights, are bending all their energies on the acquisition or the dispersal of things without

[58]

value, forever shifting worthless matter to and fro. So the two classes, misers and spendthrifts, are pictured in the fourth circle of Hell, incessantly rolling huge weights in this direction and in that, halfway around their ring, bumping into each other at their two meeting-points, and then starting back again to begin afresh.

> Descending to the fourth, from worse to worse,
>   Further adown the doleful pit we go,
>   Which bags the evil of the universe.
> Justice divine! now who hath packt below
>   The curious torments I am witnessing?
>   Why doth our foolish sin despoil us so?
> E'en as the swells above Charybdis swing,
>   Breaking against the waves they go to meet,
>   So dance the spirits in their endless ring.

One would have expected hypocrisy to arouse in Dante much the same disgust as flattery; but his reaction to it — judging from the penalty he decrees — was quite diverse. Perhaps he had encountered less of this vice in his own dealings with men, and therefore looked at it more abstractly. At any rate, what most impressed him in hypocrisy was the irony of it: the hypocrite, cloaking his evil designs in a show of righteousness, trying to impose upon his fellowmen, is constantly imposing on himself a burden greater than any that his intended victims bear — a mantle of solid lead, gilded on the outside. " Down below," says Dante, " we found a painted troop, which was marching around with steps exceeding slow, weeping, with a tired, exhausted look. They had capes with cowls lowered over their eyes, cut on the pattern that is made for the monks in Cologne. Without, they are gilded, dazzling to the eye; but inside, all of lead. . . . O endlessly wearisome mantle! We turned once more to the left, in their direction, interested in their sad tears; but those tired people, hampered by their load, came so slowly that we changed our company at every movement of the hips. Wherefore I besought my leader: 'Pray, find out someone known by deed or name; turn thine eyes about, as we walk thus!' And one of them, who caught my Tuscan speech, shouted after us: 'Stay your feet, ye who run so fast through the dark air! Haply mayst thou get from me what thou seekest.' Whereupon my guide turned and said: 'Wait, and then proceed at his pace.' I stopped, and two of them I saw showing in their faces great mental haste to be with me; but their burden and the narrowness of the way retarded them. When they were come, they looked at me askance, in silence, for a long while; then turned to each other, saying: 'This man, from the movement of his throat, seemeth alive! If they are dead, by what privilege do they walk without the covering of the heavy robe?'"

Some sins appeared to our author not only hateful, but absurd, grotesque in their perversity. Such crimes were malfeasance in public office and the misuse of churchly authority for personal profit. Grafters are immersed in a cleft full of boiling pitch, and demons, armed with forks and prongs, fish for them from the banks. How simonists are punished, Dante tells thus: " I saw all over the sides and bottom [of the valley] the livid rock full of holes, all of one size, and every one was round. . . . Out of the mouth of each projected the feet of a sinner, and his legs as far as the thick part, the rest being inside. The soles of all the feet were blazing; and that made them wriggle their joints so hard that they would have broken bands and ropes. As flame burns greasy things, flitting only over the outermost rind, so it was there from heels to toes."

The same idea of perversion we find, but without the note of mockery, in the treatment of fortune-tellers and magicians, persons who, endowed with superior intelligence, devoted it to a forbidden purpose. Having tried to look too far into the future, they are condemned to look backward forevermore: their perverse heads are twisted to the rear, as the perverse clerics are planted upside down. " Already I was all intent on gazing into the chasm which lay open, wet with tears of agony. And I saw people coming through the round valley, silent and weeping, at the pace of religious processions in our world. As my sight penetrated lower among them, each one appeared incredibly contorted between the chin and the beginning of the chest; for the face was turned toward the kidneys, and they were constrained to march backwards, since they were bereft of the power of looking to the front. It may have sometimes happened that violent paraly-

sis hath so misshapen a man; but I have never seen
it, and do not believe it occurs. Reader, as thou
hopest that God may permit thee to profit by thy
reading, now consider for thyself how I could
keep a dry face when I beheld our form, close at
hand, so distorted that the tears fell from the eyes
adown the back!"

There is another kind of perversion, — that of
the common cheat, such as the counterfeiter or the
transmuter of metals, — which provokes nothing
but unmitigated contempt and ridicule. Here are
the swindlers, disfigured by horrid disease: "The
suffering was as great as if all the sick people from
the hospitals of [malarial] Valdichiana between
July and September, and from Maremma and
Sardinia, were all gathered in one ditch; and a
stench came from them, such as comes from putrid
limbs. . . . Thus were spirits languishing, piled
up in stacks. One was heaped upon another, on
belly or on back; another, on its face, was crawling
over the doleful way. Step by step we walked,
watching and listening to the invalids, who could
not lift themselves. Two I beheld leaning against
each other, as pan is propped up against pan to
dry. From head to foot they were spotted with
scabs; and never have I seen currycomb plied by
a stableboy whose master is waiting for him, or
who is eager to go to bed, so briskly as each of
these continually plied upon himself the sharp
edge of his nails (because of the raging itch, which
has no other relief), pulling down the scurf with
his nails, as a knife doth the scales of a bream —

or of any other fish that hath still bigger ones.
'O thou that with thy fingers dost strip off thy
mail,' began my leader to one of them, ' and that
from time to time dost turn them into pincers, tell
us whether any Italian is among those who are
in here, so may thy nail suffice thee eternally for
this business.' ' Italians are we both, whom thou
seest here so wasted,' answered one of them weeping; ' but who art thou, who dost question us?'
And my leader answered: ' I am descending with
this live man down from ledge to ledge, engaged
in showing Hell to him.' At that the common support [of the two] was broken, and each one turned
to me all quivering; and so did others who caught
the word on the rebound."

No superior intelligence is here, to awaken
sympathy for these wretches; no pride of intellect
led them astray. The author shows them no such
pity as he bestows on the soothsayers.

Dante, proudly conscious of mental powers beyond the ordinary, felt himself akin to the men of
genius who were similarly endowed; and respected
them even in their downfall. The intellectual gift
which, perverted, brought the sorcerers to ruin,
was wrongfully used also by the heretics, whose
punishment is burial in a fiery tomb, and by the
evil counselors, who walk enveloped in tongues
of flame, looking, when viewed from above, like
fireflies in a valley at dusk. In these punishments
there is something that approaches dignity and
even beauty.

Upon another class of sinners, the amorous,

THE POWER OF DANTE

Dante, the great lover, could not bear to inflict a debasing penalty. After death, as in life, they are wafted helplessly before a blast that never dies.

All dumb of light the place which now I find.
　　It bellows like the sea on stormy days,
　　　When swept by striving squalls and angry wind.
The blast of Hell, which never stops nor stays,
　　The spirits on its giddy current flings,
　　　With whirl and clash tormenting them always.
As starlings oft are carried by their wings
　　In winter time, a broad and serried train,
　　　E'en so the gust the guilty spirits swings.
Here, there, it drives them, up and down again.
　　No hope of rest consoles the wraiths below,
　　　Not even hope of mitigated pain.
As cranes their doleful ditty singing go
　　And make across the sky a lengthening streak,
　　　Thus souls I saw approach, with voice of woe,
Transported by the storm whereof I speak.

LECTURE III
TEMPERAMENT

How greatly our enjoyment of an author is enhanced by the possession of his likeness and by some knowledge of his personality! We crave something concrete upon which to centre our admiration, our gratitude, our affection. When we read Homer, of whose individuality we have no knowledge whatever, we like to keep in our mind's eye some fanciful portrait-bust that has come down from antiquity. Shakspere is dearer to us for what we know of his life and looks, vague though that acquaintance be. In the case of a writer as autobiographical as Dante, the need of a tangible focus is even more pronounced than it is with an impersonal genius like Homer or Shakspere. Fortunately we have for our poet something to satisfy our want, a face that presides over our reading, an image that we may call up at will: the presentment of the youthful Florentine, left us by Giotto in the Bargello, is sufficiently authentic to fill our demand, and, at the same time, is adequate to our conception of what the author of the *Vita Nuova* should be. It is a strong and noble figure, refined, intelligent, self-contained, thoughtful but not sad. Such an Alighieri it was that Lionardo

Bruni described: " He was courteous, spirited, and full of courage; he took part in every youthful exercise; and in the great and memorable battle of Campaldino, Dante, young but well esteemed, fought vigorously, mounted and in the front rank." While he devoted himself eagerly to study, Bruni continues, he " omitted naught of polite and social intercourse. It was remarkable that, although he studied incessantly, none would have supposed from his happy manner and youthful way of speaking that he studied at all."

Another Dante face is familiar to us, the face of the death mask and of the Naples bust—a face, which, though we cannot trace it back to the man himself, is so wonderful in its power and its infinite sadness that we like to think of it as his. It tallies well with Boccaccio's account, except that, like the Giotto portrait, it is beardless. " Our poet was of moderate height," says Boccaccio, " and, after reaching maturity, was accustomed to walk somewhat bowed, with a slow and gentle pace, clad always in such sober dress as befitted his ripe years. His face was long, his nose aquiline, and his eyes rather big than small. His jaws were large, and the lower lip protruded beyond the upper. His complexion was dark, his hair and beard thick, black, and curled, and his expression ever melancholy and thoughtful." With this description Bruni substantially agrees: " He was a man of great refinement, of medium height, and a pleasant but deeply serious face.

He spoke only seldom, and then slowly, but was very subtle in his replies."

Something of Dante's life we learn from these same biographers, Bruni and Boccaccio, a little from the poet himself and from his neighbor, Giovanni Villani, the Florentine chronicler. But what we know of his external career is as nothing compared to the revelation of his inner self in his writings. It is the disclosure of the author's soul in the *Vita Nuova* and the *Divina Commedia* that makes these works so deeply significant and so exceptional. In all the nine centuries between St. Augustine and Petrarch — between the end of ancient civilization and the beginning of the Renaissance — we find in literature no other truly distinguished personality laid bare. Indeed, the writings of all time afford few such opportunities to look into the mind and heart of a really great man. Dante's work offers, then, this profound psychological interest, in addition to the comfort of faith and the charm of art.

If we had to select from the complex of Dante's nature some one dominant trait, — something that shaped his life and showed itself in all his mental and emotional habits, — we should probably call that characteristic, " intensity." He applied himself more unreservedly than other men to all he did, thought harder, felt more keenly; and that is why, after all these years, his thoughts and feelings affect us so sharply. In his make-up there was no place for laxness or lukewarmness. We have seen how he regarded those who were neither hot nor cold. Compromise he never could abide. Of his sturdy religious faith and his energetic championship of morality, I have already spoken. Let us consider some of his other qualities.

On the intellectual side, we cannot fail to note the distinctness of his concepts, his clean-cut reasoning, his strict logic. But what impresses us most, perhaps, is his curiosity. "All men naturally desire to know," says Aristotle; and with these words Dante begins his great didactic work, the *Convivio,* or *Banquet.* In a series of allegorical love-poems in honor of Lady Philosophy, the god of Love (so the author tells us) stands for study, "the application of a mind, enamored of something, to that thing." Near the close of the *Paradiso* we find the beautiful simile of the pilgrim from far Croatia who comes to Rome to see the handkerchief on which is imprinted the true image of the Saviour, and, having heard of it and thought of it for so many years, cannot look enough, but stares and stares, trying to satisfy his yearning, as long as the Veronica is exhibited. " La concreata e perpetua sete," " the inborn and everlasting thirst," was never slaked in Dante —

> The native thirst which naught can satisfy,
> Except the draught for whose refreshing gift
> The woman of Samaria did apply.

> La sete natural che mai non sazia,
> Se non con l'acqua onde la femminetta
> Sammaritana domandò la grazia.

[68]

"My eyes," he says elsewhere, "were staring fixedly to see new things, for which they are greedy." His accumulation of book-knowledge and of observation bears witness to his thirst for learning and the eagerness of his eyes. As he was one of the most inquiring of men, he was one of the most positive; and an unanswerable question was an affliction that would have been wellnigh intolerable, without the expectation of enlightenment after death. On one occasion he declares:

> No ignorance e'er battled so with me
> With craving for a thing beyond our ken
> (Unless I am deceived by memory),
> As in my thought I seemed to suffer then.

Again he speaks of his agony of curiosity being assuaged by the near prospect of an explanation. The perfect and endless soothing of that impatient " desire to know" was essential to the completeness of the joy of such a Paradise as he imagined.

To Dante's ardent study we have, besides the evidence of its results, the testimony of Lionardo Bruni, quoted a moment since; we have also that of Dante himself, at the end of the *New Life* and in the *Banquet*. He won a great reputation as a scholar. Villani, his fellowtownsman, who for political reasons may have had a certain grudge against him, says, after describing briefly his life and works: "This Dante, from his knowledge, was somewhat presumptuous, harsh, and disdainful, like an ungracious philosopher; he scarcely deigned to converse with laymen. But for his other virtues, science, and worth as a citizen, it seems but reasonable to give him perpetual remembrance in this our chronicle." Boccaccio tells us, you remember, that he "was accustomed to walk somewhat bowed," with a thoughtful expression. Dante himself says: "As I followed Virgil, I carried my forehead as one who hath it laden with thought and maketh himself like unto half the arch of a bridge." So we may picture him, as he wrestled with the knotty problem of imperfection in the world of matter; or as he meditated on the influence of the stars, and came to understand how it acts as a corrective to heredity; or as he argued with himself the question of the sanctity of vows, which, involving a covenant between a human being and the Lord, can never be altered by one party to the bargain without the consent of the other.

When reflection caused Dante to reverse an earlier judgment, his intellectual honesty prompted him to publish his new opinion. In the *New Life* he held that poetry in the vulgar tongue should be used for amatory themes alone, because this kind of verse was invented to address ladies, who cannot read Latin; but when he wrote his treatise *On Vernacular Composition* (*De Vulgari Eloquentia*), he had reached the conclusion that there was good precedent for rimes on three subjects, Love, Righteousness, and War, although for the last he could cite no example in Italian. More than once, in his journey through Heaven, he puts into the mouth of his disembodied teachers a contradiction of views formerly advanced by himself.

Beatrice elaborately disproves the theory of the
moonspots offered by Dante in his *Banquet,* and
substitutes an explanation more in harmony with
his maturer conception of the relation between
matter and spirit. She it is, also, who corrects
his previous error (contained in the same work)
concerning the respective rank of the nine orders
of angels — an error into which St. Gregory, too,
had fallen, and, after him, Brunetto Latini. In
the *Vernacular Composition* Dante had stated
with some confidence the hypothesis that the first
language spoken by man was Hebrew; but in
Heaven he learns better, from no less an authority than Adam, who assures him that his original
idiom had vanished from earth before the building of the Tower of Babel. These imaginary
communications are, of course, in actual fact, re-
tractations on the author's part. You wonder,
perhaps, why he changed his mind with regard to
Adam and Eve: I think his reason is to be sought
in a general principle which he had adopted, either
on the strength of his own observation or at the
suggestion of Horace — the principle that spoken
languages are always varying from age to age.
Not only does Dante correct his own errors; in
one canto he ventures to correct his great master,
Virgil, putting the correction, however, into Virgil's mouth: having for some reason convinced
himself that the founding of Mantua is unsatis-
factorily told in the *Æneid,* he has Virgil relate
to him circumstantially another story of the event,
attributing the origin of the city to the Theban

prophetess Manto, whose soul they have just met in Hell.

Dante was naturally a sincere, outspoken man. But certain episodes in his career put his sincerity to a severe test. A poetic love affair, probably two different affairs, after the death of Beatrice, appeared to him, in afterthought, unbecoming in a man who set himself up as a moral teacher, and he was anxious to explain away the amatory verse in question, by calling it allegorical. This desire was one of his motives in writing the *Banquet,* which is in the form of a commentary on some of his *canzoni.* The *Banquet* was never completed; and in the *Divine Comedy* the poet sternly chastises himself for his aberration. Beatrice it is who administers the rebuke, after the sudden departure of Virgil: standing in a chariot in the Garden of Eden, " ' Dante,' " she says, " ' though Virgil leave thee, weep not, weep not yet, for thou must weep for a worse wound.' Like an admiral, who comes to stem and stern to see the crews serving in the other boats, and heartens them to do their best, thus, when I turned at the sound of my name, which of necessity is registered here, I beheld, on the left side of the chariot, that lady who had erst appeared to me under a cloud of flowers cast by angels' hands; and she was gazing at me across the stream. Although the veil that descended from her olive-crowned head did not permit me to see her clearly, she continued in regal fashion, with a mien still severe, as one who speaks but holds in reserve her most stinging words: ' Look at us well! We are indeed, indeed, Beatrice! Hast thou then condescended to come to the mountain? Didst thou not know that this is the place where man is happy?' My eyes were lowered to the clear water; but, when I saw myself therein, I withdrew them to the grassy bank, such shame weighed down my brow! Thus doth the mother seem haughty to the child, as she appeared to me; for bitter is the taste of pity that is still unripe." Dante's name is " of necessity registered here" to mark his confession as his very own. The mountain of which Beatrice speaks is the mountain of discipline. At her harsh words, the angels show pity for the culprit; and with that his heart melts: " The ice that had collected about my heart turned to breath and water, and with agony issued from my breast through lips and eyes." To the angels Beatrice explains that by nature and by special grace " ' this man, in his new life, was potentially such that every happy talent would have reached marvelous fulfilment in him. But the more good earthy vigor a piece of land has, the wilder and worse it grows, if ill planted or uncultivated. For some time I sustained him with the sight of my face. Showing to him my youthful eyes, I led him toward the right quarter. As soon as I reached the threshold of the second age of man, and passed from mortal to eternal life, he took himself from me and gave himself to another. When I had risen from flesh to spirit, and my beauty and virtue had increased, I was less dear and less welcome to him; and he turned his

steps over a road untrue, following false like-
nesses of good, which carry out no promise to the
end.'" Then she turns to Dante himself: " ' In
order the more to shame thee for thine error, and
to make thee stronger, shouldst thou hear the
sirens again . . ., thou shalt hear how the burial
of my body ought to have moved thee in the opposite way. Never did nature or art present to thee
a charm equal to that fair form (now scattered in
earth) within which I was enclosed. And if this
greatest of charms so forsook thee at my death,
what mortal thing should thereafter have led thee
to desire it? Verily, at the first arrow of disappointment over elusive things, thou shouldst have
flown up after me, who was no longer of them.
Thou shouldst not have allowed thy wings to be
weighed down, to get more wounds, either by a
little maid or by any other so short-lived vanity.
The newborn birdlet waits for two or three shots,
but, surely, in vain the net is spread, and in vain
the shaft is shot, in the sight of any full-fledged
bird.' " Presently Dante, having drunk of the
water of Lethe, which effaces the memory of sin,
and of sin only, asks Beatrice: " ' Why does your
cherished word fly so far above my sight that the
more I strive, the more I lose it? ' ' In order,' she
said, ' that thou recognize the kind of doctrine
thou hast followed, and see, too, that the human
way is as far from the divine as earth is distant
from the highest whirling heaven.' And I replied
to her: ' I do not recall that ever I strayed from
you, nor have I any sting of conscience therefor.'

'If thou canst not remember it,' she answered, smiling, 'now bethink thyself how thou hast just drunk of Lethe; and if fire is argued from smoke, this forgetfulness clearly proves that there was guilt in the turning of thy desires elsewhere.'"

Thus does Dante humiliate himself and confess the temporary faithlessness which he had tried to conceal. To be sure, his avowal, though contrite enough, is not so explicit as one could wish, and still leaves room for uncertainty as to his meaning. It is doubtless as clear as he could bear to make it; to pronounce it at all, after his protests in the *Banquet,* must have cruelly tortured his pride. For Dante was very proud. I have quoted to you Villani's statement that his learning had made him somewhat scornful and that "he scarcely deigned to converse with laymen." The poet himself recognized his failing. We have already noted that, as he marches along, in the lowest circle of Purgatory, talking with the souls which, by way of penance for pride, are carrying heavy weights on their backs, he stoops as they do. " I was walking," he says, " all bent with them; " and " side by side, like oxen under the yoke, I trudged beside that laden soul." That is, he shares in their punishment. When conversing with the envious, who have their eyes sewed up, in the terrace above, he tells what he expects to suffer when he shall come to do real penance in Purgatory after death: " ' My eyes,' said I, ' shall yet be taken from me here, but only for a little while; for little have they offended by turning in envy.

Far greater is the fear that grips my soul, of the torment below; already weighs upon me the burden that is carried down there.'" Dante seems to have regarded this sin as a family trait, since he represents his great-grandfather as having done penance for it, in Purgatory, for over a hundred years. The poet believed himself to be descended from a Roman family anciently settled in Florence. The earliest ancestor he knew, his great-great-grandfather, Cacciaguida, had been a crusader and had been knighted by the Emperor. The thought of this noble forbear must have been a comfort to him in the days of exile and poverty. For he was by nature an aristocrat, contemptuous of the ignoble crowd. When Cacciaguida's soul appears to him in Heaven, he addresses it with the respectful pronoun *voi* instead of the familiar *tu;* and Beatrice, observing the harmless fatuity of her disciple, smiles indulgently. Here is the poet's comment:

> O petty human eminence of birth!
>   If thou dost gratify poor mortals' pride
>   Where human love is feeble, down on earth,
> I ne'er shall marvel more, at any tide;
>   For in that place where hunger cannot stray,
>   I mean in Heaven, I was gratified.
> Thou art a cloak that quickly shrinks away,
>   And Time goes clipping round it with his shears,
>   Unless it be patcht out from day to day.
>   [From *Dante*, p. 35.]

"The magnanimous man," says Dante in the *Banquet,* "always magnifies himself in his heart;

and the pusillanimous man, on the contrary, always thinks himself less than he is. . . . And inasmuch as a man measureth his possessions, which are so to speak a part of him, with the measure by which he measureth himself, it follows that to the magnanimous man his own possessions seem better than they are and those of others less good; while the pusillanimous man always believeth that his own things are worth little, and other people's, much." In believing that his own mental gifts were better than other men's, Dante was amply justified. It is inconceivable that such a genius should have been unaware of his superiority. We have seen how he expected — although he refrains from saying so outright — to "drive the one and the other Guido from the nest." After all, his own rating of himself was modest enough, compared with the judgment of posterity. Who nowadays would ever have heard of Guido Guinizelli or Guido Cavalcanti, charming rimesters though they were, had it not been for Dante's mention of them? Immortal reputation Dante craved and confidently expected. Of the Provençal poet Folquet de Marselha, encountered in Heaven, he makes another blessed spirit speak thus:

This bright and precious jewel of our sky,
   Which gleameth here beside me, left behind
   Enduring fame, so great that ere it die
This present year shall five centennials find.
   Strive to excel! For so thy mortal life
   A second life shall leave to humankind.

Dante himself, debating whether he shall incur the enmity of the mighty by telling the truth in his poem, declares:

> If timidly I love the truth, I fear
> I may not live among the men for whom
> Antiquity shall be the present year.

To him Cacciaguida replies, urging him to be frank, regardless of the consequences:

> No envy on thy neighbors need be spent;
> Because thy life shall flourish, stretching on
> Far, far beyond their treason's punishment.

The natural endowments of our poet, as described by Beatrice, I have read to you. His native constellation of Gemini, bestower of the gift of literary art, Dante apostrophizes thus:

> O glorious stars, O light that ever teems
> With wondrous power, to which alone I owe
> My genius (or the thing that genius seems),
> The sun, begetter of the life below,
> Did daily set with you and daily rise
> When first I felt the Tuscan breezes blow.

When Virgil returns to the Limbus, bringing with him Dante, whom he is to conduct through Hell and Purgatory, a little company of his fellow-ghosts comes to meet him.

> A sudden voice I heard exclaiming then:
> " Honor the noble poet, now be glad!
> His shade, which left us, cometh back again."
> When silent was the voice that welcome bade,
> I four majestic souls advancing see,
> Whose faces neither joyous were nor sad.

[78]

And thus my kindly master spake to me:
   "Look well on him who cometh sword in hand,
   And kinglike walks before the other three;
Homer is this, who poets doth command.
   Horace the satirist is second there.
   The third is Ovid. Lucan ends the band.
Since every one of these with me doth share
   The title which the single voice did call,
   They do me honor, as is right and fair."
Thus I beheld united, grand and tall,
   Those princes of the most exalted song
   Which like an eagle flieth over all.
Before their greetings had extended long,
   They turned to me with hospitable sign;
   And Virgil smiled, assured they did no wrong.
But, thanks to them, more glory still was mine;
   For they received me in their company,
   And I was sixth in that enlightened line.

This, then, was the place that Dante assigned himself in the hierarchy of poets: he was sixth, following Virgil, Homer, Horace, Ovid, and Lucan; perhaps ahead of Statius, the only other ancient poet whom he knew. Few critics there be, in our time, who would not put Dante at the top of the list.

That he was guilty of pride, Dante plainly tells us; and he seems to suggest that he was also somewhat prone to anger and strife, although he strongly reprobated this tendency. At any rate, in Purgatory, he is blinded and stung by the thick, biting smoke which is the punishment of the wrathful; and in Hell, not only does he gloat over a vulgar quarrel, until he draws a sharp rebuke from Virgil, but he likewise contemplates with a sort of drunken fascination the souls of mischief-makers.

These are frightfully mangled by a demon with a sword. Among them the most notable figure is that of Bertran de Born, the Provençal warrior-poet, who made his profit out of the discord between Henry the Second of England and young Henry, his eldest son, known as the Young English King. "I lingered to stare at the crowd, and saw something which, without further proof, I should be afraid to tell unaccompanied, were it not that conscience reassures me, that good companion which emboldens a man under the hauberk of conscious honesty. I surely saw, and seem to see again, a bust walking headless, just as walked the others of the sorry flock. And its severed head it held by the locks, dangling from its hand, like a lantern. He was looking at us and saying: 'Ah me!' Of himself he made a lamp for himself; and they were two in one and one in two. How this can be, He knoweth who so decrees it. When he was just at the foot of the bridge [on which we stood], he lifted up his arm, head and all, to bring nearer to us his words, which were: 'Now dost thou behold the cruel punishment, thou who, still breathing, goest visiting the dead! See whether any is as great as this!'"

Neither love of strife nor guilty anger must be confounded with righteous indignation, which the sight of sin should and does inspire in the godly. The good and the bad kind of wrath are contrasted in the fifth circle of Dante's Hell, where sinners are fighting in the Stygian pool. "I, who was absorbed in gazing, saw muddy people in that bog, all naked and with a damaged look. They were smiting one another, not only with hands, but with heads, chests, and feet, and rending bit by bit with their teeth." As Dante and Virgil are crossing the swamp in Phlegias's little boat, a dramatic incident occurs. "While we were speeding over the dead millpond, someone leaped up before me full of mud, saying: 'Who art thou, that comest before thy time?' And I to him: 'If I come, I stay not. But who art thou who art grown so ugly?' He replied: 'Thou seest, I am one who weep.' And I: 'Thy weeping and thy mourning, accursed spirit, now keep to thyself, for I know thee, filthy as thou art.' Then he stretched out both hands toward the craft. But my ready master pushed him away, and cried: 'Off, off, with the other dogs!' Then Virgil clasped my neck with his arms, kissed my face, and said: 'Indignant soul, blessed be she who bore thee! This creature was in the world a man of arrogance. There is no goodness to adorn his memory; and therefore is his shade so frenzied here. How many up yonder now think themselves great kings, who shall dwell here like pigs in dung, leaving horrible scorn behind!' 'Master,' said I, 'greatly should I enjoy seeing him ducked in this mess, ere we leave the lake.' 'Before the shore be seen,' he answered, 'thou shalt be satisfied. It is right for thee to have enjoyment of such a desire as that.' A little later I saw the soul so torn by the muddy mob that I still praise and thank God for it. 'At Filippo Argenti!' they all shouted; and the frantic Florentine ghost turned its own teeth upon itself."

Burning indignation against sin, even violent hatred of the sinner, is a frequently recurrent note in Dante's *Hell,* and is by no means absent from his *Purgatory* and his *Paradise.* Amidst the peace and perfect joy of Heaven, St. Peter breaks out into angry invective against his unworthy successor on the papal throne: "He who on earth usurps my place, — my place, my place, which is vacant in the sight of the Son of God, — hath made of my burial-ground a sewer full of stench and blood; whereat the Evil One, who fell from here, is satisfied down below." So, among the penitents on the mountain, the wicked House of France is denounced by its founder, Hugh Capet: "I was the root of that direful plant which so overshadows all the Christian earth that righteous fruit is very seldom plucked. . . . Before the great dowry of Provence robbed my race of shame, it was of little worth, but still it did no harm. Then, with violence and falsehood, it began its ravening course. Next, to make amends, it stole Ponthieu and Normandy and Gascony. Charles came into Italy, and, to make amends, sacrificed Conradin, and shoved St. Thomas back into Heaven, to make amends. . . . O my Lord, when shall I be gladdened by the sight of the vengeance, which [still] concealed, sweetens thy wrath in thy secret [heart]?"

Dante's own wrath was no doubt eased, if not sweetened, by the thought of the just punishment that awaited the enemies of God and man. Down at the very bottom of the pit, in a sheet of ice, the cold-blooded traitors freeze forever. " I saw before me and under my feet a lake which the cold made to look like glass instead of water. Never did the Danube in Austria in wintertime, nor the Don under its chilly sky, draw such a thick veil over its current as there was here; for if [the mountain of] Tambernich had fallen on it, or Pietrapana, it would not have cracked even at the edge. And as the frog sits croaking with its nose out of the water, at the time of year when peasant women are apt to dream of gleaning, so were the doleful souls in the ice, livid as far as the place where blushes come, setting their teeth to the tune of the stork. Every one held its face downward. Their [chattering] mouths bore witness to the frost; their eyes, to their sad hearts. When I had gazed about a little, I looked at my feet, and saw two [spirits] so close together that the hair of their two heads was mixed. ' Tell me,' said I, ' ye who so squeeze your breasts, who are ye?' They bent their necks; and when they had lifted their faces toward me, their eyes, which up to then had been wet only within, gushed up over the lids, and the cold congealed the tears inside them and locked them up again. Never did clamp fasten wood to wood so hard. Whereupon they, like two bucks, butted at each other, such rage came over them. And one, who had lost both his ears from freezing, said, without raising his face: ' Why dost thou stare so at us?' " The vileness of these souls makes Dante hard-hearted against them, callous and spiteful. " While we were walking toward the centre which attracts all weights, —I know not whether it was intent or fate or chance, — but, as I stepped among the heads, I kicked the face of one of them hard with my foot."

Enough of hate: let us turn to the opposite passion. Love is the source of all good and all evil; it is the motive power of the universe. In the most literal sense of the word, it makes the world go round, for it is love that causes the heavens to revolve. The noblest of emotions, the one which, at its best, lifts us up to God, may be utterly perverted, or it may be inordinately bestowed on an unworthy object. Perverted love, love of injury, is malice, the fruit of pride, envy, or anger. Inordinate love of food is gluttony; of wealth, avarice. Excessive love between men and women is amorousness. Of this fault Dante seems to confess himself guilty, not only in sundry lyrics and in various episodes of the *New Life*, — as well as in the passage I have quoted from the *Purgatorio* (the lines containing the rebukes of Beatrice), — but also in another thrilling scene in this latter book. To the poet's earliest amatory verse, addressed to various young ladies, I should not attach much importance: it may express nothing more serious than transient youthful fancies or sentimental reveries. Some intensely passionate poems apparently belonging to his mature years are very mysterious, and possibly (though not probably) written with an allegorical intention.

Beatrice's reproof, as we have seen, is a bit ambiguous. Clearer evidence of experience in forbidden love is Dante's treatment of Francesca da Rimini, whose culpable passion is handled with such sweet and delicate sympathy, and with such perfect insight, that the author cannot escape suspicion of knowing more than one should know. But in the scene of the *Purgatory* of which I spoke, there appears to be a distinct avowal.

On the uppermost terrace of the mountain, which Dante is traversing with Virgil and Statius, the souls of the amorous are cleansing themselves by marching through fire, which bursts out from the cliff all around the peak. Among them are the love-poets whom the author most esteemed, Guido Guinizelli and Arnaut Daniel. To leave this shelf, where Dante has been walking on the outer edge in order to avoid being scorched, he must penetrate the wall of flame — that is, he must submit to the burning, and clean his soul, even as the penitential ghosts are attaining cleanness. And now we encounter a trait that we have not previously met in Dante: rebellion against the purifying discipline, reluctance to abandon his vice. In the circle of pride, he spontaneously joined in the penance; but here, far from diving voluntarily into the fire, he stubbornly resists the exhortations of Virgil, who represents Reason. " The day was departing when God's glad angel appeared to us. Outside the flame it was standing, on the brink, singing ' Blessed are the pure in heart ' with a voice far more alive than ours. When we had come near, it spake: 'Ye may go no further, blessed souls, until ye suffer the bite of the flame. Enter into it; and be not deaf to the song on the other side.' At these words, I felt like one who is put into the grave [to be buried alive]. Straining forward over my clasped hands, I stared into the fire, distinctly picturing human bodies that I had formerly seen burnt. My kindly escorts turned towards me, and Virgil said: 'My son, here may be torment, but not death. Remember, remember! If I guided thee in safety even on [the back of the monster] Geryon, what mayst thou not expect of me now, nearer to God? Believe for certain that, though thou shouldst abide a thousand years and more in the heart of this flame, it could not strip thy head of one hair. And if thou thinkest perhaps that I am deceiving thee, approach it, and with thine own hands convince thyself, with the hem of thy garment. Now put aside, Oh! put aside all fear! Turn hither, and step fearlessly ahead!' But I [stood] stubborn, disobedient to conscience. When he saw me standing hard and obstinate, he cried, a little troubled: 'Now see, my son, this wall is between thee and Beatrice!' As Pyramus, at the point of death, opened his eyes on hearing Thisbe's name, and looked at her, — on the day when the mulberry turned red, — thus, with my hardness all softened, I turned to my wise leader, hearing that name which is ever green in my memory. Whereupon he shook his brow, saying: 'How now! shall we linger here?' as one does to a child won over by an apple. Then he plunged into the fire ahead of me, begging Statius to bring up the rear. . . . When I was within, I could have thrown myself into molten glass to cool me, so boundless was the heat. My dear father, to encourage me, continually spake of Beatrice alone, as he advanced, saying: 'Already I think I see her eyes.' We were guided by a voice that was singing on the other side; and, fixing all our attention on it, we came forth to the upward way."

In this incident we may see, I think, allegorically related, the rescue of Dante from an unworthy passion by the memory of his pure affection for Beatrice. What was this guilty love? Perhaps his entanglement with the girl at the window; perhaps his mad infatuation with the woman he calls Pietra, for whom he wrote those wildly beautiful amatory poems of which I spoke. To two ladies, it would seem, his heart was temporarily given, after the death of the most gentle one. One is this mysterious Pietra. The other is a young girl whom we may perhaps name Lisetta: the lady who, in the latter part of the *New Life*, so moved the poet by looking at him compassionately from a window — the same one whom he afterwards made a symbol of Philosophy. Some critics believe that these ladies are one; others think that there is yet a third, the woman of the Casentino, celebrated in Dante's "mountain song"; others still would add a fourth, a certain Gentucca, but there is really no reason whatever for thinking that she was an object of Dante's affection. Let us assume that there are but two, the sympathetic Lisetta and the stony Pietra. From his undue interest in the former he was saved, according to the account in the *New Life,* as follows: " Against this adversary of reason there arose one day, almost at the ninth hour, a powerful fancy within me; for I thought I saw this glorious Beatrice with those vermilion garments in which she had first appeared to my eyes, and she seemed to me a child of like age to that in which I first beheld her. Then I began to think of her; and, as I meditated on her, following the order of past events, my heart began painfully to repent of the desire by which it had weakly allowed itself to be possessed for some days, contrary to the steadfastness of reason; and, casting out this evil desire, all my thoughts turned back to their most gentle Beatrice."

Now, the episode of the barrier of fire and the magic effect of the name of Beatrice would seem to be a symbolical presentation either of this same experience with the so-called Lisetta or of another passage of similar kind, perhaps with the dangerous Pietra. That Dante regarded Beatrice as in very sooth his saviour there can be no doubt. At first, perhaps, — in Dante's adolescent stage, of which we catch faint glimpses through the mist of idealization which veils the *New Life,* — he looked upon her with eyes of youthful admiration and longing, though from a respectful distance; but ere the narrative is half over, we find the poet banishing from his devotion to her every element of desire and confining his song to the note of praise. This platonic, spiritual service developed into a veritable cult, which after the lady's death was only intensified, and always remained as an uplifting influence, comparable to that of the Blessed Virgin. Beatrice it was who, watching over him from Heaven, saved him again and again from his lower self; and it is not strange that his feeling toward her should have come to be one of overwhelming gratitude, and that he should in his allegorical thought have made her the symbol of divine guidance.

Of all Dante's emotions, I am inclined to think that gratitude was the strongest. Grateful he was, first of all, to God—to the Creator who made this wonderful universe and so lovingly watches over it—to the Redeemer who, in preference to any other method of restoring lost humankind, chose to make reparation by sacrificing himself. God's grace it is that floods the heavens with light and happiness and beauty. Of Satan's ugliness the outstanding cause is ungratefulness to his Maker. Among all the human sinners in Hell, the three worst—Judas, Brutus, and Cassius—are guilty primarily of ingratitude. It was Dante's thankfulness to God that made him so unsparingly vehement in his denunciation of the wicked. Gratitude to his earthly teachers, living or dead, finds eloquent expression in his verse: to Virgil, his great master, whom he chooses as his director and companion for the journey through Hell and Purgatory; to Brunetto Latini, his sage counselor, to whom he pays such touching tribute; to the ancient author of his Latin grammar, Donatus, whom he places in Heaven among the great lights of religion; to the literary models whom he followed, Arnaut Daniel and Guido Guinizelli. Passage after passage of the *Divine Comedy* testifies courteously, discreetly, but with transparent sincerity, to his thankfulness toward those who had befriended him during his exile.

Courtesy, good breeding marked his dealings with his fellowmen. "His manners," says Boccaccio, "whether in public or at home, were wonderfully composed and restrained, and in all his ways he was more polite and civil than anyone else." Nothing could be more delicate than Dante's compliments to benefactors, unless it were his words of comfort to suffering penitents. We have observed how loath he is, in Purgatory, to walk, staring and silent, past a row of repentant spirits who, temporarily blinded, cannot look at him. A very pattern of refinement, with a tincture of sedate playfulness, is the colloquy between Virgil, Statius, and, as an unwilling participant, the poet himself. In his relations with his friends we note the same sweet delicacy. He does not in any of his works say much about friendship; the theme was perhaps too intimate to come within the bounds prescribed by his code of behavior. Yet in his occasional mention of Guido Cavalcanti, his "first friend," of that unnamed relative of Beatrice who was next in the order of friendship, of Cino da Pistoia, his fellow-poet, — in his meeting with Guido's father in Hell, with the musician Casella on the shore of the mountain, with Forese Donati in Purgatory itself, with Charles Martel in Heaven, — we have evidence of that considerate tenderness which makes friendship beautiful. This same tender, deferential feeling exists between two of Dante's shades, who have just met for the first time, but have long loved each other from afar. Virgil, who has come from the Limbus, to be the poet's guide, meets Statius in Purgatory, in the circle from which the latter has just been released — the circle which contains both the avaricious and the prodigal. " ' Love,' began Virgil, ' love, kindled by virtue, hath always kindled love in return, whenever its flame could show itself. And that is why, ever since Juvenal came down among us, in the Limbus of Hell, and told me of thy affection for me, my liking for thee hath been the greatest that ever bound one to a person unseen — so great that these stairways [which we are to climb together] will now seem to me all too short. But tell me (and forgive me as a friend, if over-assurance gives me too loose a rein, and as a friend now explain to me), how could avarice find a place in thy breast beside all the wisdom with which thy zeal had filled thee?' These words made Statius smile a little at first; then he answered: ' Every utterance of thine is a precious token of love to me. Verily ofttimes things do occur which offer undue occasion for misgiving, because the true reasons are hidden.

Thy question discloses to me thy belief that I was avaricious in the other life, perhaps on account of the circle where I was. Now learn that avarice was too remote from me, and this immoderateness hath been punished during thousands of moons. . . . Therefore, if I have been among those people who weep for avarice, it hath befallen me for the opposite cause.'" And Statius goes on to relate that his salutary repentance for this sin was aroused by meditation on the hidden meaning of a passage in Virgil's *Æneid*.

If friendship is too personal a sentiment to discuss, we must not expect to meet in Dante much exhibition of the still more sacred affections of family life. Never, in all his works, does he mention his wife or his children; yet no one ever wrote more sympathetically of the mother surrounded by her little ones, or of the emotions of the young child. Look for no lengthy descriptions of household scenes: you will find only the rapidest of sketches, thrown in from time to time by way of simile; but these sketches bear witness to a close and loving observation. Let me prove it by a few examples:

Awaking late, no little innocent
   So sudden plunges toward its mother's breast,
   With face intent upon its nourishment,
As I did bend.

And as a babe, which stretches either arm
   To reach its mother, after it is fed,
   Showing a heart with sweet affection warm,
Thus every flaming brightness reared its head.

TEMPERAMENT

With that expectancy I turned aside
  With which a little child to mother runs,
  Whene'er he is distrest or terrified.

I turned, all dumb with wonder, to my guide,
  Just as a child, who runs his woes to tell
  Always to her in whom he doth confide;
And, as the mother comforteth full well
  And quickly, too, her pale and panting boy
  (That voice of hers doth all his fears dispel) . . .
                    [From *Dante,* pp. 314–315.]

Dante is rather fond of noting maternal affection
in birds:

As mother stork above the nest doth stir
  In loving circles, when her young are fed,
  And they, all satisfied, look up at her . . .

Let us end with the famous picture of the Florentine wives of the good old times:

One watcht beside the cradle in the night
  And, soothing, spake that language infantile
  Which first doth fond parental ears delight.
Another, swiftly spinning all the while,
  With tales of Trojans, Fiesole, and Rome
  Her troop of tiny listeners doth beguile.
                    [From *Dante,* p. 314.]

L'una vegghiava a studio della culla;
  E, consolando, usava l'idïoma
  Che pria li padri e le madri trastulla:
L'altra, traendo alla rocca la chioma,
  Favoleggiava con la sua famiglia
  De' Troiani, di Fiesole e di Roma.

LECTURE IV

EXPERIENCE

IN the preceding lecture I spoke of Dante's temperament, his traits of character. These characteristics were vigorously reinforced by the vicissitudes of his career, which also afforded various opportunity for his gift of quick and precise observation. Whatever life Dante might have led, he would have always been an interesting personality; but without the emotions, the trials, the hardships, the changes through which he passed, his genius could never have realized to the full its potential development. He learned to know the extremes of love and hatred, of happiness and misery, of joyous expectation and sad retrospect. To Dante himself, even more than to Virgil, his teacher, apply the immortal words of Francesca.

> Ed ella a me: " Nessun maggior dolore
> Che ricordarsi del tempo felice
> Nella miseria; e ciò sa il tuo dottore."

The Florence of the latter thirteenth century was a good city to live in. Virtually independent, busy, eagerly ambitious, she was attaining, in her manufactures, her trade, and her political influence, a foremost place among the little munic-

ipal republics of Italy. Newly acquired wealth
enabled her ancient civilization to break into
fresh flower: the refinements of courtly society
were easily adopted by her sturdy commercial
population: the arts — architecture, painting,
music, poetry — were cultivated with all the zest
of novel interest, with all the delight of hitherto
unknown achievement. Florence was sufficiently
big to lend distinction to any sort of local supremacy among her citizens, and occupations were so
diversified as to afford opportunity to competence
of any kind; on the other hand, the closely packed
town was small enough, and gossipy enough, for
everyone of any account to be known to everyone
else. The conditions, as you see, were favorable
to the unfolding of talent. And talent did unfold,
during those decades, to an extraordinary extent.
Internal politics, to be sure, occupied much of the
burghers' attention, changes of government were
frequent, and party strife sometimes led to blood-
shed. There was a strong reactionary group of
old-time aristocrats, discontented with the modern
democratic tendency, willing to resort to any
means to maintain their ascendency over the despised commoners; there was an energetic middle
class, well organized in guilds, which, having
gained control of most of the property and power,
was bent on reducing the old nobility to impotence
and substituting for it a new aristocracy of wealth;
there were the laborers, important on account of
their numbers, who sided now with one party, now
with another, having no consistent policy. Family

rivalry, too, ran high. Indeed, the factional violence which finally threw Florence into the waiting hands of the Pope, and brought about Dante's exile, appears to have had its origin in the social competition of the Donati and the Cerchi, the former being leaders among the blue-bloods, the latter preëminent among the new-rich.

Until he was about thirty years old, Dante, it would seem, did not concern himself with politics. Belonging to a family of modest possessions but with some claim to gentle extraction, he was well educated, well bred, and apparently mingled with the socially elect; at any rate, he appears to have been affianced in childhood to one of the Donati clan, whom he married in due time; and he had as an intimate associate another offshoot of this stock, Forese Donati. His closest friend was Guido, a distinguished member of the very rich Cavalcanti family, who had great influence in the progressive party. Guido, a man of independent views, was a poet of real merit, and also something of a philosopher and scholar. Other friends of young Alighieri were the notary Lapo Gianni and the jurist Cino da Pistoia (both of them excellent rimesters), the musician Casella, and, according to report, the architect and painter Giotto. It was, you see, an artistic *milieu*. Even Forese Donati wrote verses; and that unnamed brother of Beatrice, whom Dante calls second among his friends, was evidently fond of them. Dante himself early conceived a passion for poetry, and devoured the songs of southern France and the imitations of them made in Italy. Thus he " found out for himself " — so he tells us — " the art of composing things in rime." Among the Provençal troubadours, the one whom he most admired was Arnaut Daniel, a brilliant master of technique; among the Italians, his favorite was Guido Guinizelli of Bologna, who introduced the spiritual, symbolistic treatment of love. By the time he was eighteen, Dante had won some local reputation as a poet; and before he was thirty, his fame had gone abroad to other cities. His youthful verse did service to various damsels of his Florence, but especially to one whom he calls Beatrice, probably Beatrice Portinari, the daughter of a well-to-do neighbor. Very sweet and dainty are these early poems. As an example, let me cite this ballad:

Chorus

The memory of a garland
Shall always make me sigh
Whene'er I see a flower.

I

One day I saw thee, Lady, wearing
    A tiny garland, fresh from Maying;
And over it a fay was faring,
    A modest little love-sprite, swaying,
        With cunning music saying:
        " Whoso shall me espy
Shall praise my master's power."

The memory of a garland
Shall always make me sigh,
Whene'er I see a flower.

[97]

II

If I, O floweret sweet and fairest,
　　Come close enough to see thee twining,
" My Lady," I shall say, " thou wearest
　　My sighs upon thy head reclining."
　　　　But then, to prick my pining,
　　　　My Lady shall come nigh
　　　　New-crowned from Cupid's bower.

　　　　The memory of a garland
　　　　Shall always make me sigh
　　　　Whene'er I see a flower.

III

My curious little words to fashion
　　A ballad out of flowers have striven,
Stealing, to decorate their passion,
　　A garment once to others given.
　　　　I beg thee, then, by Heaven:
　　　　What man the song shall try,
　　　　Give him thy richest dower.

　　　　The memory of a garland
　　　　Shall always make me sigh
　　　　Whene'er I see a flower.

[From *The Ladies of Dante's Lyrics,* pp. 38–39.]

I have already discussed Dante's feeling toward
Beatrice. It is not easy to define; but, whatever
it was, it was profound and sincere, and her death,
which occurred when he was just twenty-five,
affected him as a grievous loss. Yet during her
lifetime he had shown a good deal of interest —
at least in a poetic way — in several other young
ladies; and at different periods after her departure
he seems, as we have noted, to have been in love

[98]

with two other women. One of these he turned into an allegorical figure of Philosophy, as he had made Beatrice a symbol of divine revelation. We cannot be sure that he ever allegorized the other, the irresponsive Pietra. Here is a characteristic stanza from one of the later love-poems:

I cannot flee from her, nor yet prevent
    Her coming to my mind;
  Nor yet from thought, which brings her there, refrain.
My crazy soul, on self-destruction bent,
    Still pictures her, unkind
  And beauteous as she is, and thus repeats its pain;
  Then looks on her once more, and full again
Of boundless longing, drawn from witching eyes,
Against itself it cries,
  Which lit the fire that burneth it to death.
  All reason's checks and arguments are vain
When raging whirlwinds in my bosom rise!
My anguish, loath to bide within me, flies
  Forth from my lips so plain, men hear its breath,
  And eyes to pay their tribute summoneth.

[From *The Ladies of Dante's Lyrics,* p. 100.]

Even if Lionardo Bruni and Dante himself had not spoken of the poet's pursuit of knowledge, we should have guessed from his works that he was an insatiable student. His great passion for learning came after the death of his lady, and lasted throughout the rest of his life. He mastered the philosophers and theologians of the Middle Ages and all the classic Latin literature that was accessible; grammar, logic, rhetoric he acquired, astronomy and mathematics, such history and geography as he could get; and we may infer from a curious passage in the *Paradiso,* describing an experiment with a light and three mirrors, that he even attempted some investigation of his own in physics. He certainly learned much of music and painting; and he read pretty extensively in the vernacular literature of France and Italy. It is very odd that he nowhere mentions a noted contemporary scholar in a neighboring city, Albertino Mussato of Padua, author of a Latin play on the tyrant Ezzelino da Romano, the first tragedy in modern letters. Nowhere does he speak of the most famous French work of the Middle Ages, a poem written in his own century, known in part to his master, Brunetto Latini, and very cleverly paraphrased in Italian at about the time of Dante's marriage — the *Romance of the Rose.* This paraphrase, by the way, is so admirable that some have actually ascribed it to Dante himself. For these omissions we cannot account.

How Dante supported himself, either before or after his exile, is a question for which the answer is lacking. His father, apparently, had been a notary; but we do not know that the son had any profession. In early childhood he lost his mother; and his father, after marrying again, died while Dante was still a boy, leaving him with the charge of a half-sister and a half-brother, in addition, it would seem, to an own sister. When a little over thirty, Dante wedded Gemma Donati, by whom he had four children, two boys and two girls. We know nothing whatever of his domestic life, except that when he went into banishment, his family did not accompany him, although at the close of his pilgrimage three of his children were living near him in Ravenna. We do know, also, that he somehow got into financial difficulties in Florence, accumulating a debt that was not paid until after his death. It is hard to resist the temptation to associate this experience with Dante's repeated insistence on the wickedness of prodigality. Both in Hell and in Purgatory, you remember, this fault is put on a par with avarice. The Latin poet Statius, who seems in some respects to be a copy of the author, is represented as having been a spendthrift; he it is that laments the ignorance which prevents men from recognizing that prodigality is a sin and from correcting themselves in time to escape damnation.

At about the date of his marriage, Dante went into politics. He had previously done his duty as a soldier, in a campaign against the Aretines. Inasmuch as the new constitution restricted important office to members of guilds, Dante entered the corporation of doctors and apothecaries, which included also booksellers and painters. It was a rich, powerful guild, and it probably contained some of Dante's good friends. He was elected to two popular city councils, was a member of a special committee, and was sent on a mission to San Gemignano; but although we find an occasional record of a vote or a speech by him, we know next to nothing of his share in public affairs until he became a Prior in 1300. There were six

Priors, who formed the principal executive branch
of the government; they held office for only two
months, and could not be immediately reëlected.
In political matters, Dante's sympathies were
divided. As an enthusiastic champion of municipal independence, he naturally sided with the
bourgeois party, called the Whites, who were
opposed to papal control of the city. As a gentle-
man and an associate of the Donati, — who were
leaders of the Blacks, — he must have disliked
the crudeness of the dominant middle class and
deplored their attempt to suppress the aristocracy.
He had friends on both sides of the house —
Guido Cavalcanti with the Whites, Forese Donati
with the Blacks. The latter died, however, in
1296.

For the opinion of the ordinary run of men,
Dante had little respect. He was no democrat.
"The common people," he says in the *Banquet*,
"are for the most part bereft of the light of dis-
cretion, because, being engaged from the beginning
of their lives in some business, they necessarily
so turn their minds to it as to think of naught
else. And since the use of any moral or intellectual virtue cannot be acquired suddenly, but
must be won by practice, and they put their practice in some trade, without concern for other
things, it is impossible for them to have judgment.
They are to be called sheep, not men. For if one
sheep should throw itself from a cliff a thousand
paces high, all the others would go after it; and
if one sheep for any reason gives a jump while

crossing a road, all the others jump, though they see nothing to jump over." In the *New Life,* after having explained one of his poems, he adds: " I admit that for the further disclosure of the meaning of this ode, a more minute analysis would be required. But, nevertheless, if there be any persons of insufficient wit to understand it with the analysis already given, I should not be sorry to have them let it alone; for really I fear I have conveyed its meaning to all too many people by analysing it as I have — provided it should come to pass that many should have an opportunity to hear it." Literature is for choice spirits alone — not for Master Martin or Mistress Bertha. So it is with science, morals, government: only the enlightened, the competent should presume to guide. Of his own competence Dante had no doubt. You know the old anecdote which represents him as saying, when Florence was to select someone for a difficult mission: " If I go, who remains? and if I remain, who goes? " I do not believe this story: in the first place, because anecdotes hardly ever are true; in the second place, because I think Dante was too well-bred to make such a remark. But he may very well have thought it.

Determined our poet was to rise above the vulgar herd, to attain a high place even among the exalted. Ambition was unmistakably a directing force in his life. It is interesting to note how he portrays the souls of ambitious men in Heaven. You recall how pale and feeble are the images of

weak-willed spirits in the moon — the class of the
blest that is content with the lowest degree of
happiness. Now, the ambitious are, in the scale
of beatitude, the next-to-lowest; but how different
they look to Dante's eye, as he comes among them
in the midst of the planet Mercury! Like a school
of fishes approaching the surface of a still pond,
he sees more than a thousand bright forms advancing through the light, all of them crying:
"Lo! here is one who shall add to the sum of our
love!" And, as each one draws near, the poet
can discern the glad soul within the clear effulgence
that issues from it. "Think, reader," he continues, "if that which is now beginning should not
go on, what an agonizing hunger thou wouldst
have, to learn more, and thou shalt see for thyself
how eager I was to hear from these spirits what
was their state, as soon as they became visible to
my eyes." One of the pious throng bids him put
his question, and Beatrice cries: "Speak, speak!
and believe them as thou wouldst believe creatures
divine!" "I see clearly," responds the poet,
"how thou dost nestle in thine own gleam, and
how thou dost shoot it from thine eyes; because
they sparkle so when thou smilest. But who thou
art I know not, nor why, worthy soul, thou hast
the degree of that planet which is veiled from
mortals by the sun's rays." "Thus I spake, looking at the light that had first addressed me.
Whereupon it grew far brighter than before. As
the sun, which, after its heat hath consumed the
thick, tempering mists, hideth itself with its own

excessive blaze, even so, as its joy increased, this holy figure concealed itself within its own rays, and thus, all enveloped, it answered me." The spirit is Justinian, who proceeds to narrate the glorious history of Rome.

Distinction came to Dante with his elevation to the Council of Priors; but it was an honor full of peril. The early summer of 1300 was a critical moment. A papal plot had been unearthed in the city, three Florentine conspirators had been caught, and the new Council inherited the dangerous task of executing the severe sentence passed on the culprits. The Pope, who had been breathing fearful threats against Florence, sent thither as an ostensible peacemaker Cardinal Matteo d'Acquasparta. Bloody street-riots ensued. Thereupon the Priors ordered out of the city the chiefs of both factions, among them Guido Cavalcanti, Dante's first friend. The government's decree was obeyed by the Whites, and Cavalcanti died of a fever contracted during his short banishment; but the Blacks, trusting to the cardinal, remained. At this point Dante's term of office expired, and we have every reason to believe that he went to Rome with the vast army of pilgrims who were drawn there by the great papal jubilee. Religious excitement thus followed close upon an exhausting political strain. It is in this jubilee year of 1300 that Dante puts the action of his *Divine Comedy*. The next spring found Dante a member of an electoral commission; presently he is charged with the supervision of alterations in a street. We learn that he spoke several times, once in opposition to the cardinal, who had demanded a hundred horsemen. Pope Boniface, meanwhile, had worked out a plan to gain possession of Florence: Charles of Valois, brother of the French king, was invited by him to occupy the city and reconcile the contestants. Quick to see the significance of this move, the Florentines sent a delegation, — of which forlorn hope Dante was probably a member, — on a fruitless mission to plead with the Pope. During their absence, Charles entered Florence and gave it over to the Blacks, who sacked the houses of their adversaries. Boniface appointed a mayor of his own, and the city became for a time a part of the papal domain. The cardinal, on his return to Florence, set about devising, in conjunction with the new mayor, the total destruction of the independent party which had opposed him.

In January, 1302, a number of recent officials, among them Dante, were accused of various crimes and condemned to fine, two years' exile, and confiscation of their goods. They were summoned also to appear before the court within three days; and, as none of them were foolish enough to comply with this command, they were in March sentenced to death by fire. A persecution of the other Whites ensued; and at last Charles of Valois, having completed his work, took his leave. He is treated in the *Divine Comedy* with a scorn almost beyond words. "Without weapons he issues forth alone, with the lance with which Judas tilted;

and with that he pricks so well that he bursts the belly of Florence. Thereby shall he win not land, but sin and shame, which shall weigh on him the heavier, the more lightly he esteems such mishap." The plotter who was at the bottom of the mischief, Pope Boniface VIII, the poet represents not only as a dishonest prelate but as a shameless usurper, for whom a place in Hell was waiting when Dante journeyed below. "Art thou already standing there," cries a lost soul, planted upside down in a hole in the rock, on hearing Dante speak, "art thou already standing there, Boniface? The writing [of destiny] hath lied to me by several years. Art thou already cloyed with that pelf, for the sake of which thou didst not fear to wed by trickery our fair lady [the Church] and then to despoil her?"

It is now possible to understand Dante's hatred of treachery — a hatred which at first shocks the modern reader. Traitors are at the very bottom of his Hell, embedded in ice; and, far from showing them any mercy, he has a right good will to pay them in their own coin. So he does with a certain Friar Alberic; this villain had caused his guests to be murdered, at his own table, by assassins who, concealed behind the tapestries, sprang out at the signal: "Serve the fruit." Listen to the poet's story: "One of the sufferers in the frigid crust cried out to us: 'O souls, so cruel that ye are sent to the last station, remove from my face the stiff veil [of ice] so that I may vent the grief which steeps my heart, for a little while, until the tears freeze up again!' And I replied: 'If thou wouldst have me help thee, tell me who thou art; and then if I relieve thee not, may I have to go to the bottom of the ice!' At that he answered: 'I am Brother Alberic, he of the fruit of the evil orchard, who here am getting date for fig.' 'Oh!' said I to him, 'art thou then dead already?' 'How it may be with my body in the world above,' said he, 'I have no knowledge. This [region of Hell called] Tolomea hath the privilege that ofttimes the soul falls here before Atropos gives it the push. And, to make thee readier to scrape from my face the glassy tears, I tell thee that, as soon as a soul betrays as I did, its body is taken from it by a demon which afterwards directs it until its [allotted] time shall have revolved, while the soul plunges down into the tank. Perhaps there is still to be seen above the body of that shade which is wintering here behind me. Thou must know, if thou hast just arrived down here. He is Master Branca d' Oria, and several years have gone by since he was thus confined.' 'I believe,' said I, 'that thou deceivest me, for Branca d' Oria hath never died; he eats and drinks and puts on clothes.' 'Not yet,' was the reply, 'had [his victim] Michel Zanche reached the ditch of Badpaws, higher up [in Hell], where the sticky pitch is boiling, when this man left in his body a devil in his stead; and so did one of his kinsmen, who committed the act of treachery with him. But now stretch out thy hand hither, open mine eyes!' But I did not open them for him. And it was kindness to be harsh to him."

After the condemnation of March, 1302, Dante was a wanderer on the face of the earth. "Ever since it was the pleasure of the citizens of Florence, that most beautiful and famous daughter of Rome, to cast me out of her sweetest bosom, in which I was born and bred up to the middle point of life, and in which, with their good will, I yearn with all my heart to rest my tired mind and end the time allotted me," says Dante in the *Banquet*, "[ever since then] I have traveled through nearly all the regions over which our language extends, a stranger, almost a beggar, displaying against my wish the wound of Fortune, for which the blame is ofttimes unjustly put upon the wounded one. In truth I have been a ship without sail or helm, carried to various harbors and inlets and shores by the dry wind which blows from grievous poverty." "As Hippolytus went forth from Athens," declares the prophetic speech of Dante's ancestor, Cacciaguida, "so must thou go forth from Florence. This is willed, this is already devised, and soon shall be accomplished by him who contriveth it in the city where Christ is daily bought and sold. The blame shall follow the injured party, in report, as it always does; but the punishment shall bear witness to the truth, which dispenses it. Thou shalt leave behind all things most dearly loved; and this is the arrow which exile's bow first shoots." In the envoy of one of his odes, the poet cries: "O my mountain song, thou goest forth. Haply shalt thou see Florence, my city, which, void of love and bare of pity, locks me outside."

In 1311 Dante was expressly excluded from a proclamation of amnesty, and in 1315 his sentence was renewed. A letter attributed to him explains why he had rejected a pardon offered on condition that he pay a fine and do public penance. Still, from beginning to end, he probably never abandoned altogether the hope of restoration. In the first years of their misfortune the banished Whites banded together, concentrating principally in Bologna, and left nothing undone to regain their homes: they sought help from earlier exiles, they appealed to cities hostile to Florence. In 1303 and 1304 there were unsuccessful military attacks. Failure begat recrimination and dissension; and Dante, turning his back on his fellow-outcasts, formed, as he said, a party by himself. Five or six years later, a dazzling new hope arose, to be followed by bitter disappointment. In 1309 Henry of Luxemburg was crowned Emperor with the title of Henry VII, and, soon after, came down into Italy to restore peace, order, and justice. Henry was an idealist, a firm believer, like the poet himself, in the divinely ordained function of the Empire. Sundry Latin letters, written at this time, show Dante almost mad with enthusiasm and impatience. What he suffered we can imagine, when in 1313 his hero died, without having fulfilled his mission. A throne is reserved for the Emperor in Heaven. "On that high seat upon which thou bendest thine eyes because of the crown above it, shall sit," says Beatrice, " ere thou sup at this marriage banquet, the soul of mighty Henry, imperial on earth, who shall come to straighten Italy before she is ready. The blind greed that bewitches mortals hath made them like unto the babe, which, though dying of hunger, driveth away its nurse." One hope remained: perhaps his poetic fame would move his fellow-citizens to open their gates to him. "If it ever come to pass," writes Dante in his *Paradiso,* "that my sacred poem, on which Heaven and earth have set their hand, so that it hath made me lean this many a year, overcome the cruelty which locks me outside the pretty fold, — where I slept as a lamb, hated by the wolves that attack it, — with a changed voice at last, with a changed fleece, I shall return a poet, and over my baptismal font shall receive the crown." An invitation to Bologna, with expectation of a laurel wreath, the poet courteously rejected, still putting his faith in Florence, which was stubborn to the end.

During his twenty years of exile, Dante, as far as we know, was a dependent, living for the most part on the bounty of the great, to whom he rendered such service as he could. "Thou shalt learn," prophesies Cacciaguida, " how salty is the taste of other men's bread, and what a hard road it is to climb up and down other men's stairs." No doubt he met with many humiliations during those weary years when, in his own words, " he brought himself to quiver in every vein." Rivalry

he surely had to encounter, unworthy self-seeking,
envy, "that bawd which never hath turned her
lusting eyes away from Cæsar's house," envy,
"death of all mankind, and vice of courts." No
wonder indignation became with him an habitual
mood and condemnation his wonted solace. I
have spoken of the loathsome fate of flatterers in
his Hell. Money-lenders fare but little better.
Sitting under a rain of fire, disfigured beyond
recognition, they are distinguishable only by the
coats of arms on the money-bags dangling from
their necks; for they are gentlemen of good birth,
all Florentines but one. " Out of their eyes gushed
their grief. First here, then there, they kept up
the defense with their hands, now from the flames,
now from the hot ground. Even so do dogs be-
have in summertime, with snout and foot, when
they are bitten by fleas or gnats or flies. On the
faces of some of them, on whom the painful fire
descends, I set eyes, but recognized not one. I
observed, however, that from the neck of each
hung a pouch with a certain color and a certain
design; and their eyes seemed to feed on these."
One of them speaks to the traveler; and " at that
he twisted his mouth and stuck out his tongue, like
an ox licking its nose."

Still lower in the human scale is the snake-like
thief. Even thieves are sometimes of genteel
stock. Listen to the horrible doom of two of
them, who appear to Dante, — the first shaped
as a man standing beside a companion, the second
as a four-legged serpent, — and slowly exchange

their forms. " As, under the heavy scourge of dog-days, the lizard, changing its hedge, looks like a flash of lightning when it crosses the road, thus, darting toward the bellies of the other two [shades], there came a fiery little snake, livid and black as a peppercorn. First it pierced, in one of them, that spot where the human babe first receives nourishment; then it dropped down outstretched before him. The pricked one stared at it, saying nothing, but yawning, with feet motionless, as if sleep or fever were upon him. He glared at the snake, and the snake at him, both of them sending out a thick smoke, the one through his wound, the other through its mouth; and the smokes met. . . . Keeping time together, this is what they did. The serpent split his tail into a fork. The wounded man pressed his legs tight, one against the other; and shins and thighs so grew together that in a little while the line of joining could no longer be seen. The cleft tail took the shape that was disappearing in the other body. Its skin softened, and the skin of the other hardened. I saw the arms shooting in through the armpits, and the reptile's two little front feet lengthening just as the man's arms shortened. While the smoke shrouded both of them in a strange color, generating hair on one head and stripping it from the other, the first stood up, the second dropped down, neither for a moment averting his evil gleaming eyes, under which the snouts were changing. The upright one slid his muzzle back toward the temples, and, out of the superabundant matter which was drawn thither, ears emerged from the smooth cheeks; as much of that superfluity as remained, instead of running back, made a nose on the face, and thickened the lips to the proper extent. The prostrate one projects his snout, and slips his ears into his head, as a snail pulls in its horns; and the tongue, which was whole and fit for speech, is cleft, while the other's forked tongue is closed up. And the smoke stops. The soul transformed into a beast flees hissing through the valley; the other is left behind to speak and spit."

Such was the impression made on Dante by many of the types of humanity that he encountered on his wanderings. All sorts and conditions of men he must have met, from " the mountaineer, who comes to town all rough and wild, and silently stares in open-mouthed confusion," to the haughty lordlings who " think themselves great kings, but after death shall be as pigs in dung, leaving behind them on earth horrible contempt." The hunter he knew, who "wastes his life watching for little birds;" the " modern prelate, who has grown so great that he needs some one to prop him on either side, and some one to lead, and some one to hold him up behind, while he covers his palfrey with his mantle, so that two beasts go marching under one hide;" the gambler, who in failure and in success is thus depicted: " When the game of dice breaks up, the loser is left behind to repine, going over the throws again, a sadder and wiser man. But all the gang goes off with the other, one walking in front of him, one plucking at him from behind, one beside him claiming his attention. He forges ahead, hearing this one and that, [from time to time] stretching out his hand to some one of them, who then drops out of the press; and thus he escapes from their crowding." "O witless striving of mortals," exclaims the poet in his *Paradiso,* " how faulty are the arguments that make thy wings flutter downwards! One man was chasing after law, another after the *Aphorisms* [of Hippocrates]; one was pursuing priesthood; another, power, by means of violence or sophistry; one, robbery; another, municipal business; one was wearing himself out, entangled in the pleasures of the flesh; another was devoting himself to idleness — while I, liberated from all these things, in company with Beatrice, was so gloriously welcomed in Heaven above!"

It would have been sad indeed if Dante, in his long banishment, had seen nothing but wickedness and folly, if the only note awakened by his experience had been one of reprobation. Happily he found also courtesy and kindness, recognition of his talent, fame and respect, generous hospitality, to which his grateful nature was quick to respond. Contentment was never his, for he could be satisfied with nothing short of rehabilitation in his native city; but his last years seem to have been in the main placid, if not cheerful. Sweet to him was the thought of benefits received, and a delight it was to record the names of benefactors. Some of these names would have perished utterly, had he not saved them from oblivion. What do we know of the young hostess Gentucca, save that she made the Tuscan city of Lucca dear to Dante, in spite of its evil repute? Who would remember the name of Alagia dei Fieschi, married to Moroello Malaspina, had she not entertained our wanderer in the Lunigiana, in northwestern Italy? Of her the shade of her uncle, Pope Adrian V, speaks thus in Purgatory: " I have a niece yonder, called Alagia, good by nature, if only my house make her not wicked by its [bad] example; and she is the only one I have left [to pray for me] on the other side." Little report has come to us of " good Gherardo," who was in fact Captain General of Trevigi, in the northeast, a member of the powerful family of Camino, but of whom the poet implies that he is sufficiently identified by adding the epithet " courtly " to the adjective " good," habitually applied to him. He is one of the three old men who still represent, in upper Italy, the gentle breeding of past genera- tions. " In the country watered by the Adige and the Po," says Mark the Lombard, " goodness and courtesy used to dwell, before [Emperor] Frederick had his quarrel [with the papacy]; but now that land may be fearlessly crossed by anyone who shall have forsworn, through shame, all com- pany and converse with the righteous. Neverthe- less, there still remain three old men, a rebuke of the former age to the present; and the time seems long to them ere God restore them to a better life [above]: Corrado da Palazzo and good Gherardo and Guido da Castello, of whom it is better to speak, in French fashion, as ' the honest Lombard.' "

To and fro Dante must have journeyed, in central and northern Italy. His presence is attested in Padua and in Venice. At some time he surely studied in Bologna. It is barely possible even that he went to Paris, as Villani and Boccaccio affirm. But for the most part his routes and his stations are unknown. We are sure of this much, that he was hospitably received in Verona by Bartolomeo (or perhaps Alboino) della Scala in 1303 or 1304; by Moroello Malaspina in the Lunigiana in 1306; in Verona again by Can Grande della Scala; and in his last years by Guido Novello da Polenta, nephew of Francesca da Rimini, in Ravenna, "where the Po descends to find peace from its pursuers." To the families of Malaspina and la Scala — and especially to Can Grande — he pays fine tribute. Why, in his extant works, he has no praise for Ravenna, the Polenta clan, or Guido Novello, his last host, I cannot guess. It was in Ravenna that Dante died in 1321.

A Latin letter, ostensibly by Dante and probably authentic, dedicates the *Paradiso* to Can Grande, to whom the first canto is sent with this document. The epistle is thus addressed: " To the magnificent and victorious lord, Lord Can Grande della Scala, Vicar General of the most holy Roman Empire in the city of Verona and the town of Vicenza, his most devoted Dante Alighieri, a Florentine by birth but not in character, wishes a life happy through time everlasting and a perpetual increase of his glorious name." The letter begins by declaring that the author was attracted to Can Grande's court by its far-spread and almost unbelievable fame. "There did I behold your greatness, there did I both see and feel your kindness; and whereas I had previously suspected exaggeration on the part of those who had told thereof, I now learned that the exaggeration was on the part of the facts themselves. And so it came to pass that having already been, from report alone, a respectful well-wisher, I became at first sight a liegeman and a friend." Dante's earlier sojourn in Verona is thus prophesied by Cacciaguida: "Thy first refuge and thy first inn shall be the courtesy of that great Lombard who bears [on his coat of arms] the sacred bird [of Empire] at the top of the ladder. He shall have for thee such considerate regard that — between you two — of doing and asking, that one shall come first which, among others, lags behind." In Verona Dante is to see Can Grande, at that time a boy of nine, of whom Cacciaguida foretells momentous things, "things incredible even to those who shall behold them."

Another Latin epistle, generally accepted as really Dante's, is addressed "to Lord Moroello, Marquis of Malaspina." To prove what ties of gratitude bind the servant to the master, and to counteract any false accusations of neglect, the author has decided to bring this communication before His Magnificence, now that he has parted from that court for which he has yearned ever since. The letter serves as a preface to one of Dante's odes, a love-song written in the Casentino. On the mountain of Purgatory, among the princely shades waiting in a dell, there is a member of this same hospitable and valiant family. "'I was called Conrad Malaspina,'" it says. "'I am not the elder, but am descended from him. On my own people I bestowed that love which here is being purified.' 'Oh!' said I to him, 'never have I been in your lands. [This was in 1300.] But where in all Europe do men dwell who know them not? The fame that glorifies your house proclaims the masters and proclaims the county, so that he who never yet was there hath heard thereof. And I swear to you, as I hope to go on high, that your honored clan is still beautiful with the glory of purse and sword. From habit and nature it hath such advantage that, however the wicked chief may twist the world awry, it alone walketh straight, despising the wrongful way.'" Thereupon the spirit prophesies that ere seven years be gone, Dante's friendly opinion shall be confirmed by experience.

The admiration that Dante professes for such distant courts he is far from bestowing on Florence or the neighboring cities. These get little but the hottest invective. His burning indignation against them would seem, however, to be oftener objective than personal, kindled by hideous crimes or notorious sins of their inhabitants, rather than by injury to himself. After listening to the piteous story of Count Ugolino, who with his sons and grandsons was left by the Pisans to starve in the Hunger Tower, he exclaims: "Ah! Pisa, accursed of the peoples of that fair land where *sì* resounds, since thy neighbors are slow to punish thee, let [the islands] Capara and Gorgona bestir themselves and make a dam across the Arno's mouth, that it may drown every human being within thee!" The godless thief, Vanni Fucci, declares in Hell: "A beast am I, and Pistoia was the right lair for me." "Ah! Pistoia, Pistoia," cries Dante, "why dost thou not decree to burn thyself to ashes, since thou dost outstrip thine own seed in evil?" The sight of Branca d' Oria, the traitor and murderer from Genoa, moves the poet to a similar apostrophe: "Ah! Genoese, strangers to all morality, full of all corruption, why are ye not scattered from earth?" Bologna is a nest of panders, Lucca a hotbed of bribery. A devil in Hell comes rushing down to the stream of boiling pitch, bearing on his shoulder an official from the latter city. "From our bridge he shouted: 'O Badpaws, here is one of the aldermen of Santa Zita! Shove him below! I am going back for more, to that town which I have abundantly supplied with them. Everyone there is a grafter, except Bonturo. There you can turn *no* into *yes* for money.' He flung the sinner down, and, turning back over the rugged ridge, was swifter than a mastiff let loose on a thief. The soul plunged under [the pitch], and came up with arched back. Whereat the demons, beneath the bridge, shouted: 'Here is no place to pray to the Holy Face! The swimming is not like the river Serchio! Therefore, if thou likest not our hooks, do not show thyself above the pitch!' Then they snapped him up with more than a hundred prongs, saying: 'Here all the dancing is under cover. Do thy grabbing unseen, if thou canst!' Even so do cooks bid their scullions push the meat under, with their forks, in the middle of the pot, to keep it from floating." In the portrayal of these mischievous guardians, wickeder than the criminals they torment, and, as Dante and Virgil nearly learn to their cost, quite as ready to punish the innocent as the guilty, there seems to be a bit of personal reminiscence; for in them the poet probably intended to picture with grim humor the unscrupulous officials of Florence who accused him of dishonesty and condemned him to death by fire.

Toward Florence, the beautiful ingrate, Dante's feelings were mixed. Florence was his city, his "pretty fold," for which he always yearned; yet Florence was foolish, presumptuous, fickle, cruel, the home of glib and shallow politics. Terrible are his repeated denunciations and his prophecies of coming retribution. "But a little while hence," he cries, "thou shalt suffer what [thy neighbor] Prato wishes thee — not to speak of others. If it had already happened, it would be none too early. Would it might be thus, since it must be! For it will be the harder for me to bear, the older

I grow." All along the Arno, declares a soul in Purgatory, from its mountain source to its mouth, " virtue is shunned as a foe by all as if it were a snake, either because of some ill fortune of the place, or because evil custom incites them; therefore have the dwellers in that wretched valley so changed their nature that one would think Circe had put them to pasture." The people of the Casentino are ugly swine, fit only for acorns; the Aretines are curs, who snarl louder than their strength justifies; the Florentines are wolves; the Pisans foxes, so full of deceit that they fear no trap.

From the wickedness and stupidity of men Dante turned for comfort to the perfect goodness and wisdom of God. Always of a genuinely religious bent, he became, in the days of adversity, more deeply devout, more ardent and mystical in his aspiration. With intense meditation on things divine, came unexpected divine illumination.

> Then suddenly did day redouble day,
>   Or so it seemed, as if the One who can
>   Had bid the sky a second sun display.

In very truth Beatrice might have said to him, as she cries in the poem:

> Thou art not, as thou thinkest, down on earth;
>   For lightning never left its native sky
>   So swift as thou dost seek thy land of birth.

Faithful as Dante was, and eager to conform his will to the will of the Almighty, his intellectual curiosity and his positive, logical mind made it

EXPERIENCE

difficult for him to leave a mystery unexplained.
Theological study fascinated him, and he evidently found in it satisfaction for most of his
speculative difficulties. One problem, however,
always baffled him: the origin of imperfection. At
least, although he returns to it again and again,
he never reaches a consistent solution. The material world, he says, is defective because, being
made of matter, which is by nature imperfect, it
cannot fully realize God's perfect idea. This
explanation suffices for a Platonist, who holds that
God and matter are coeternal, but not for a Christian, who believes — and, if orthodox, must believe — that matter was created by the Lord.
Indeed, this doctrine of the creation of matter is
explicitly stated by Dante, who affirms also that
whatsoever God himself has made is perfect. So
we are left where we were in the first place. If it
were possible to assume that matter has always
existed, we might argue further that, not being
the work of the Creator, it is inferior, and that
whatsoever is fashioned of it must fall short of
perfection. But this assumption is heretical.
Here is a sore temptation for a philosopher,
divided between his faith and his logic. Dante
himself, as he tells us in the *Banquet,* was dis-
turbed by the question "whether the primal matter of the elements was conceived by God." He
decided aright; but his experience enabled him to
sympathize with those minds whose acumen and
self-confidence led them into heresy. The heretics
in his lower world are tormented but not despic-

able. One of the poet's most impressive figures is Farinata degli Uberti, who amid the flames "stands with brow and chest erect, as if he held Hell in great contempt." In his Heaven Dante places, among the lights of theology, two men of dubious, or more than dubious, orthodoxy: Joachim of Calabria, the mystic prophet; and the daringly brilliant philosopher Sigier of Brabant, who in the University of Paris "syllogized invidious truths."

Against unbelief he was fortified, as he was saved from the consequences of his besetting sins, by divine watchfulness, for which he never could be sufficiently thankful. A special debt of gratitude he bore to the Blessed Virgin, the embodiment of heavenly mercy, to whom he so often and so happily appealed. His devotion to her certainly influenced his whole conception of Beatrice, as it is developed in the *Divina Commedia*. When this "most gentle lady," — about to answer a really simple question which to Dante seems hopelessly difficult, — when Beatrice

> First breathed a pitying sigh, then sweet and mild
> Inclined her eyes upon me with the look
> A mother gives to her delirious child,

we see the very image of the compassionate Lady of Heaven, "the Rose in which the divine Word became flesh" — "that beauteous flower," says the poet, "on which I always call at morn and eve."

" 'Now look,' " cries St. Bernard, whom Dante

finds at his side when he reaches the real Paradise,
" ' now look into the face that is most like Christ,
for its brightness alone can prepare thee to see
Christ.' Over her I saw descending such a shower
of gladness, borne by the holy minds [of angels],
created to flit through those heights, that whatsoever I had seen before did not hold me rapt in
such amazement, nor reveal to me such likeness of
God." To her the saint addresses that beautiful
prayer beginning

> Vergine madre, figlia del tuo Figlio,
> Umile ed alta più che creatura,
> Termine fisso d' eterno consiglio,

which continues thus: " Thy kindness not only
succors him who asks, but ofttimes freely forestalls
the asking. In thee is mercy, in thee piety, in thee
magnificence, in thee is united whatsoever goodness there is in aught created. Now this man,
who from the lowest pool of the universe as far
as here hath beheld the spiritual states one by
one, beseeches thee, in thy grace, for such power
that his eyes may lift him still higher toward the
Last Weal. And I, who never yearned more
hotly for my own sight than I now long for his,
offer thee all my prayers — and I pray they be
not scant — that thou, with thine own supplica-
tions, melt from him every mist of his mortality,
until the Joy Supreme shall be revealed to him.
Further I pray thee, O Queen, who canst do thy
will, to keep his desires whole, after this great
vision. Let thy watchfulness overcome his human

impulses. Lo! Beatrice and all the blest are
clasping their hands to thee, joining in my
prayer!"

> Those eyes which God doth love and venerate,
> Upon the suppliant bent, revealed to us
> How dear to her are those who supplicate.

LECTURE V
VISION

"O IMAGINATION," cries Dante, "which at times dost so abstract us from the outer world that a man heeds it not though a thousand trumpets blare about him, who kindles thee, when the sense offers thee naught? Art thou kindled by a light that takes shape in Heaven, either by itself or by a will which directs it downward?" Is it a chance ray from the stars, or is it the mysterious purpose of the Lord, operating through their beams, that suddenly flashes a picture before the mind's eye? Whether the gift come from nature or from God, it is in some measure transmissible from man to man. The poet not only sees visions but has the power of clothing them in words and thus communicating them to others. This gift was possessed in the highest degree by Dante. The reading of his poem is like a dream of magic pictures — pictures clear and beautiful, but momentary, crowding one another in their swift, ceaseless eddies, while the deep current of thought rolls on below. For most readers of Dante nowadays, this lightning play of description constitutes his principal charm.

Not a few of his sketches are evidently sug-

gested by his reading, many more by his experience
of men and things; some would indeed seem to have
been flashed into his brain by the stars. Now and
again we find a scene, drawn by him in his own
way, but born of a general impression derived
from some book ancient or modern. Virgil's
Elysian Fields are probably the prototype both
of the Noble Castle, — which shelters the great
spirits of pagan antiquity in Dante's Limbus,
shining bright and peaceful in the midst of the
dark air a-quiver with sighs, — and of the Valley
of the Princes, flowery and sweet in the lap of the
mountainside of Purgatory, peopled by shades of
recent rulers. Dante's Garden of Eden is made
up of features common in legend — trees, flowers,
birds, streams — but invested with new loveliness
by Dante's phrasing and with new interest by his
introduction of the sweet maiden, Matilda, the
embodiment of eternal springtime. It is one
thing to say, as the old stories do: "There did
they behold wonderful trees, which never lost
their leaves; and marvelous birds, singing songs
not heard on earth; and miraculous flowers covering all the ground; and four beautiful rivers," and
quite another thing to write such a passage as
Dante's

> Vago già di cercar dentro e dintorno
> La divina foresta spessa e viva,
> Ch' agli occhi temperava il nuovo giorno,
> Senza più aspettar, lasciai la riva,
> Prendendo la campagna lento lento
> Su per lo suol che d' ogni parte oliva.

VISION

Impatient now the mysteries to spy
  Within the thick and lusty forestland
  Which screened the rising sunshine from the eye,
Awaiting naught beside, I left the strand,
  Advancing slowly, slowly 'mid the trees
  O'er turf that fragrance breathed on every hand.
A gentle wind, which, never changing, flees
  Eternally, was blowing on my brow,
  But blowing softly as the softest breeze;
And, quick to quake, the leaves on every bough
  In that direction all inclining went
  Where casts its shade the holy mountain now;
But not enough from their uprightness bent
  To still the birds that in the tree-tops stay
  All fearless, on their highest art intent.
With glad, full-throated song, the coming day
  They greeted 'mid the twigs in music clear,
  While rustling leaves accompanied their lay.
Such burden we from branch to branch may hear
  Throughout the grove of pines on Chiassi's shore,
  When Æolus Scirocco sends anear.
So far within the ancient woodland's core
  My lingering steps had carried me that I
  The spot from whence I came could see no more,
When lo! a brook forbade my going by,
  Which toward the left, with tiny ripples, pried
  The grass which all along its bank did lie.
The purest rill that runs on mountainside
  With us, would some uncleanness seem to show
  Compared to that, which naught doth ever hide,
Tho' shady, O! so shady it doth flow
  Beneath undying green, which not a ray
  Of sun or moon will e'er admit below.
My feet did halt, and yet mine eyes did stray
  Beyond the streamlet, gazing, wondering
  At all the fresh and varied gifts of May;
And then appeared to me, — as doth a thing
  Which unexpectedly its face hath shown

> Make for amazement every thought take wing, —
> A lady walking through the field alone,
>   Singing and plucking, choosing flower from flower
>   Amid the tints wherewith her path was strewn.

Hell, as well as Eden, has its traditions. In other visions of the lower world, as in Dante's, there is a graded immersion in ice; but there are no "faces grinning doglike," and the author does not "forever afterwards shudder at the sight of frozen pools." In the apocryphal Vision of St. Paul there are murderers plunged to different depths in a fiery river; but we miss the "shrill shrieks of the boiled" as we walk "along the edge of the boiling red." Brother Alberico speaks of a fiery breath blowing spirits before it; but it is an unpoetic breath, with no suggestion of "starlings borne along by their wings, in cold weather, in a broad, close array" nor of "dirge-singing cranes making a long streak of themselves in the air," and it does not blow in a place "dumb of all light."

> Now I begin the doleful notes to hear
>   Not far away from me, for I am come
>   Where cries of grief abounding smite mine ear.
> The place I reach, of every light is dumb,
>   And bellows like the storm-tormented main
>   When warring winds on ocean's surface drum.
> The never-ceasing hellish hurricane
>   Sweeps on the spirits in its circling swirl,
>   Turning and clashing them in endless pain.

Oftener than a whole scene, it is some rapid little sketch that stirs Dante's fancy and moves him to free imitation. Such is the landslip de-

scribed by Albertus Magnus and added by our
poet to the topography of Hell: "That slide
which smote the flank of Adige, slipping down
from the mountaintop in such fashion as to afford
a sort of path to anyone who might be above."
Such the little boat, which, both in Virgil's lower
world and in Dante's, feels the unaccustomed
weight of a human body, and "cuts deeper into
the water than is its habit." Such is the figure
of David, dancing "with all his might" before
the Ark of the Covenant, and his wife "Michal
Saul's daughter," who "looked through a window,
and saw king David leaping and dancing before
the Lord, and . . . despised him in her heart."
Such is Satan, falling "as lightning from heaven."
Frequently, as in this last case, it is one word or
brief phrase that has stamped itself on the poet's
imagination. If, in Statius's *Thebaid*, the "fat
clouds" had not obstructed Mercury's progress,
Dante's angel, who comes to his rescue before the
City of Dis, walking dryshod over the Styx, would
not be "fanning from his face the fat air, busily
swinging his left hand before him." If the book
of *Great Derivations,* the nearest approach to a
dictionary that our poet knew, had not given to
the word *hypocrite* the fantastic etymology *super-
auratus,* "gilded outside," the "whited sepul-
chers" in Dante's Hell might have escaped the
punishment of crushing leaden cloaks, covered
with gold externally. We wonder why Dante's
giants are placed, not with those who did violence
to God, but far below, around the mouth of the

last pit of Hell — until we recall Virgil's words
in the *Æneid:* "Here that ancient race of earth,
the Titan brood, struck down by the thunderbolt,
roll *in the lowest depth.*" The Griffin in Dante's
Garden of Eden, the creature of two natures,
which symbolizes Christ, has "limbs of gold, in
so far as it is bird, and the rest of white mixed
with red," even as the "beloved" in Solomon's
Song, who is also a symbol of Christ, "is white
and ruddy," and "his head is as the most fine
gold." Lucan tells of flocks of cranes, which,
"as chance directs, shape various patterns," but
"when the wings are dispersed, the *broken letter*
fades;" and so the bright souls in Dante's Heaven
of Jupiter, — "like birds which rise from a river-
bank and, as if rejoicing together in their feast,
make themselves now into a ring, now into some
other figure, — flitted singing, and took the form
now of D, now of I, now of L, first tuneful and
moving to their own music, then, having turned
into one of these letters, lingering a little while
in silence:" thus they spell the sentence from the
Book of Wisdom, "Diligite justitiam, qui judi-
catis terram," "Love justice, ye that be judges of
the earth." On the shore of Dante's lonely island,
it is just before sunrise, on Easter Sunday, that

> The dawn was driving out the early breeze,
>   Which ran so quick ahead that far from shore
>   I recognized the rippling of the seas;

but Virgil's "sea that gleams beneath a quivering light" is a nocturne. A troubadour, Bernart
de Ventadorn, once sang thus of the lark:

VISION

The little lark that full of mirth
　　Up, up the sunbeam winged her way
Forgets herself and drops to earth,
　　With heart enraptured by her lay.

The same bird, in the *Divine Comedy*, is tuneful,
then silent, like her Provençal prototype:

The little lark that singing, soaring went
Is silent now, and craveth naught beside
The last sweet note which made her heart content.

Our poet's elderly counselor, Brunetto Latini,
following a line of naturalists modern and ancient,
describes in his *Trésor* an Indian monster called
Manticore, which has a man's face, a lion's body,
a scorpion's tail, and eats human flesh. This
animal, with a suggestion from the man-faced and
scorpion-tailed locusts of the Apocalypse, became,
in Dante's hands, the dragon Geryon, genius of
fraud, which comes floating up through the air
at the edge of the abyss.

"Behold the creature with the pointed tail,
　　Which crosses mountains, shatters plate and wall —
　　The one whose stench makes all the world to ail."
These words to me my guide begins to call;
　　Then bids the beast ashore, with beckoning hand,
　　Hard by the dike whereon our footsteps fall.
That image foul of Fraud then came to land,
　　And beacht upon the brink its head and breast,
　　But never drew its tail upon the strand.
Its face was like a man's, and of the best
　　(Benevolence its skin did never quit),
　　But serpentlike its trunk and all the rest;
Two paws and arms, all hairy to the pit.
　　With shapes of knots and little rings were lined
　　Its back and sides and belly, every bit.

[133]

THE POWER OF DANTE

More colors ne'er did Turk or Tartar wind,
  Nor paint the warp and woof of carpet more;
  Arachne such a pattern ne'er designed.
As skiffs at times are left projecting o'er,
  Partly in water, partly in their place, —
  As yonder, on the greedy Teutons' shore,
The beaver takes his seat, the fish to chase, —
  E'en thus did that disgusting beast depend
  From off the rock that doth the sand encase.
In empty space its wriggling tail did bend,
  Twisting on high the poison-laden fork
  Which, scorpion-fashion, armed its very end.

On the back of this monster Dante and Virgil
descend into the pit.

Upon those ugly shoulders I alight,
  And try to say — but utterance never came
  As I expected: "See thou hold me tight!"
When I was mounted, he (the very same
  Who oft in danger held me safe and fast)
  With clasping arms sustained my frightened frame.
"Now, Geryon," he cried, "set forth at last!
  Retard thy fall, thy spiral course expand.
  Remember what a novel load thou hast!"
Just as a parting skiff is pusht from land
  And backs and backs, thus Geryon withdraws;
  Then, finding empty space on every hand,
He turns his tail where erst his bosom was,
  Stretches it out, and wriggles like an eel,
  And paddling pulls the air with both his paws.
No greater fear did Phaëthon once feel
  When, losing Phœbus' reins, he baked the sky,
  As all the Milky Way doth still reveal, —
Nor Icarus, when heat did liquefy
  The wax, and pluckt the pinions from his back,
  His father shrieking: "Badly dost thou fly," —
Than mine is now, perceiving that our track
  Lies only thro' the air, where nothing shows,

Beside the beast, but one unbroken black.
Slowly the creature smoothly swimming goes;
  And naught betrays his round descending crawl,
  Except a gentle wind which upward blows.
Now on my right I hear the waterfall
  Make under us a terrifying din;
  So I project my eyes with head and all.
But seeing fires and hearing wails begin,
  More timidly the monster I bestride
  And, all a-quiver, draw my body in.
And now I mark our circling downward ride,
  Unseen before, at last revealed to sight
  By torments pressing near on every side.
As falcon, after long and fruitless flight,
  Uncalled by lure or bird, doth downward start,
  The while his owner sighs: "Thou wilt alight,"
Wearily stoops, whose going was so smart,
  Wheeling a hundred times, and, cross and fell,
  Far from his master perches all apart,
So Geryon alighted there in Hell,
  Beneath the ragged rock's enfolding ring.
  His passengers unloaded in the well,
He sped away like arrow-notch from string.

          [From *Dante,* pp. 356–357.]

And all this mixture of stupendous fancy and vivid realism owes its inception to a terse, prosaic description of a preposterous animal by a parcel of "nature-fakers."

One of these, Brunetto Latini, at the beginning of his allegorical *Tesoretto*, relates that he "strayed in a strange wood." You all know what grew out of that haunting phrase:

    Nel mezzo del cammin di nostra vita
      Mi ritrovai per una selva oscura,
      Chè la diritta via era smarrita.

> Midway along the road that mortals go
>   I found myself within a forest drear,
>   From off the pathway I had wandered so.
> Ah! what a tearful thing to tell is here —
>   This rough and wild and woody wilderness,
>   Which, even at the thought, renews my fear!
> So bitter 't is that death is nearly less!
>   But I the good which there I found would say,
>   And so the other sights I must confess.
> I cannot rightly tell what made me stray,
>   So full was I of sleep precisely then
>   When I forsook the veritable way.

For his description of the earth and other bodies, as viewed from the constellation of Gemini, Dante had a more extensive model in the "Dream of Scipio" in Cicero's *Republic*. Like Dante, the young Scipio finds in heaven a great ancestor, a warrior; and both dreamers look back through space. Yet really, aside from the general situation, the two accounts have little in common. Cicero was a moralist, Dante a poet. "Gaze down," says Beatrice, "and see how much world I have already brought under thy feet."

> With that I turned and downward peered a while
>   Through all the seven spheres, and saw the earth
>   So small, its cheap appearance made me smile.

He sees the upper surface of the moon, which has no spots; he sees the sun and, close to it, Mercury and Venus; he sees Jupiter between Mars and Saturn; and comprehends their varying orbits.

Then showed to me the seven, star by star,
 How big they be, how rapid is their flight,
 And how unthinkably remote they are.
The little plot for which we fiercely fight,
 As I was turning with the deathless Twins,
 All met, from hills to river-mouths, my sight.

" Lower thine eyes again," says Beatrice, after
an interval, " and see how thou hast revolved."
His revolution with Gemini has described an arc
of 90°: on one side, beyond Cadiz, is the "mad
course of Ulysses " over the Atlantic; on the other,
the Phœnician shore, whence Europa departed on
the bull's back. More of the earth's surface he
could have seen, had the part lighted by the sun
exactly coincided with his field of vision; but that
was not the case, the poet being in Gemini and
the sun in Aries — or, as he puts it, " the sun,
beneath my feet, was ahead, more than a constellation away." Now of all this clearly conceived and fascinating detail there is virtually
nothing in Cicero: at most, a phrase of his may
have suggested Dante's " hills and river mouths."

It was Dante's habit, when he borrowed, to
contribute much more than he took. His famous
simile of the " mother-doves, at affection's call,
returning through the air to the dear nest, with
wings outspread and still, carried by their desire,"
was suggested, to be sure, by some lines in the
Æneid; but Virgil's dove has in common with
Dante's only the motionless wings: she is flying
away from her nest, not towards it, nor is she
" carried by desire " — which, of course, is the

THE POWER OF DANTE

feature that lends the little picture its supreme
distinction. Similarly, our poet's " autumn leaves
which drop one by one until the branch beholds
all its garments on the ground" owes to Virgil
only the dropping leaves, the pathetic fancy of
the stripped branch being Dante's invention.
Boëthius once wrote of the " rivers Tigris and
Euphrates breaking from a single spring, and
then, with severed waters, parting company."
And in Dante's Garden of Eden there are two
streams issuing from one source, which remind
the author of the classic rivers:

> Euphrates I, and Tigris, seemed to see
> From out a single fountain gushing there
> And parting, *like two friends,* unwillingly.

Here again the human touch is the work of the
later poet.

In the transformations which go on in Dante's
snake-pit, — where Ovid is his model, — the element that is added is not sympathy but horror.
The *Metamorphoses* tells of two bodies growing
together into one, but the way of telling is curious,
even pretty, rather than awful, with its " ivies
entwining the tall tree-trunks " and its "mixture
of two bodies fusing, and a single face spreading
over them both." Look at the other picture.
Dante and Virgil are gazing down into a ditch
where thieves are punished; a group of three
human figures gathers at the bottom of the bank;
and Dante, hearing the name of one of the sinners
pronounced by chance, lays his finger across his

lips, " from nose to chin," to solicit Virgil's attentive silence.

> If, reader, thou be tardy to admit
> What I shall tell, 't will be no great surprise,
> For I, who saw it, scarce believe in it.
> As I was staring down with all my eyes,
> A snake six-footed grabs a man and flings
> Itself all over him and firmly ties;
> Its middle feet around the belly brings,
> And with its forward ones the arms doth seize,
> And both the cheeks with fangs extended stings.
> Its hinder feet embrace the thighs and knees.
> Goes crawling up, along the back, its tail,
> Thrust in between the legs with piercing squeeze.
> Never so tight on tree did ivy trail
> As twines the hideous beast, whose clutches pin
> Monster to man, and limb to member nail.
> Like melting wax, they mingle, skin to skin;
> The face of one the other's color learns.
> Now neither looks like what it once has been:
> As up a piece of paper, when it burns,
> A sort of brownish tint precedes the flame,
> And neither white nor black the color turns.
> The other spirits watch, and both exclaim:
> " Agnello, thou 'st become a thing unknown,
> Nor one nor two, nor other nor the same!"
> Two heads already into one had grown;
> Two faces, dual now no more, combined,
> Fusing their features, into one alone.
> Four strips into a pair of arms entwined,
> Belly and chest and thighs and shins and face
> Became such parts as nature ne'er designed.
> Remained of former likeness not a trace:
> Both two and none the gruesome figure seemed.
> And then the thing moved on, with sluggish pace.

Carved in marble, in Dante's Purgatory, is the story of the humility and the justice of the Emperor Trajan, an incident which the poet found, much as he relates it, in medieval legend.

'T is Emperor Trajan's form that next appears,
And, near his rein, a widow in distress,
Whose attitude betokens grief and tears.
And all around him horsemen crowd and press
And eagles wrought in gold, on banners tall,
Are flapping in the wind (the eye would guess).
The mourner seems to say, among them all:
" My heart is broken, for my son is slain.
For punishment, my Lord, on you I call! "
" Now wait a bit till I return again,"
He answers. " O my Lord," she seems to moan,
As one impatient from insistent pain,
" If you return not? " " He who holds the throne
Shall do thee justice." " What shall profit you
Another's justice, who forget your own? "
" Be comforted," he cries, " for I must do
My duty ere I take another step.
Not only justice calls, but pity, too."

In this instance, Dante's source was religious and popular. More frequently, however, the spark that fires his imagination comes from the classics — oftenest from Virgil, Ovid, Lucan, or Statius. These suggestions from the Latin poets are most apparent in the *Hell,* least in the *Paradise.*

Now let us drop all the cases in which there seems to be, however remote, a literary model. We have seen, even in the partially imitative examples hitherto considered, how abundant are Dante's own resources. He was a dreamer, to be sure; but he was also, like Théophile Gautier, a man for whom the outer world exists. And it existed, for him, in no vague, indeterminate shape, "without form and void," but clear in construction, precise in outline, vivid in color, quick in meaning. When he looked at nature or at man, his eye, like that of a Japanese artist, caught the salient, peculiar traits, and stored them in a memory which let nothing fade. A touch or two, and the whole likeness is revived in his mind and conveyed to ours. Keen observation of reality is characteristic of the Italians, and still more so is the habit of stating experience, physical or mental, in terms of things seen — of attaching a visual image to the idea or the phrase. At times, Dante names the places whence his mental pictures came. The conduit running across the fiery desert in Hell is compared to the dikes built by the Paduans along the Brenta, to protect them against flood when the snows melt on the mountains. The uncanny wood of the suicides is a development of the image of the wild Maremma, in Tuscany, between Cecina and Corneto.

"We came meanwhile," he says, in the *Purgatorio,* "to the foot of a mountain; here we found the cliff so steep that legs would have there been agile to no purpose. Between Lerici and Turbia [along the Italian Riviera, Turbia being just above Monte Carlo] the loneliest, most deserted path is a plain and easy stairway, compared to this."

Here we have a scene from home: " The angel led us to a spot where the precipice was cut; then waved his wing over my brow, and promised me a safe journey. The bank, which comes down abruptly from the terrace above, is eased here — just as, on the right, to climb the hill where sits the church [of S. Miniato] (overlooking the well-governed city [Florence] beyond the Rubaconte bridge), the bold sweep of the ascent is broken by stairs," made in the good old days when men were honest.

It is altogether likely that the poet was in Rome, with countless hosts of other strangers, in 1300, the year of the great papal jubilee. At any rate he tells us how, in this emergency, the Romans, to prevent a block on the crowded bridge of Sant'Angelo, hit upon the plan of making people turn to the right. Two files of sinners, in Hell, are moving in opposite directions, " as the Romans, on account of the enormous throng, in the jubilee year, found an expedient to get people over the bridge; for on one side they all have their faces toward the Castle [of Sant' Angelo] and are going to St. Peter's, while on the other edge they are going toward the hill."

Portraying a cleft full of boiling pitch, in which grafters get their due, Dante recalls the Arsenal of Venice, famous throughout Europe for many centuries. " As in the Arsenal of the Venetians, in wintertime, the tenacious pitch is boiling, to coat their unsound craft, — for they cannot navigate, and, instead, one is building a new boat, one is calking the sides of a vessel that has made many a trip, one is hammering at stem, one at stern, one is making oars, one twisting ropes, another patching foresail or mainsail, — thus, not with fire but by divine contrivance, thick pitch was boiling down below, and making either bank all sticky."

The poets have to climb up a great cliff through a narrow crevice in the rock: "Ofttimes, in the season when his grapes are ripening, the farmer hedges up with a single pitchforkful of his briars a wider breach in his fence than was the passage through which my leader, and I after him, mounted alone, when the company had left us. Men scramble up to San Leo, men get down to Noli, men scale the summit of Bismantova, with their own feet; but here a man has to fly — I mean, fly with the feathers and swift wings of great eagerness, following that guide who gave me hope and light. Up we climbed through the split rock, squeezed by the wall on either side; and the footing below called for both hands and legs. When we had emerged on the upper rim of the tall precipice, on the open ledge, 'Master,' said I, 'which way shall we go?'"

Another ascent through another crack — this time at the entrance to Purgatory — evokes no explicit local reminiscence: "We were going up through a rifted rock, in a cleft that turned to this side and to that, like a wave advancing and retreating. 'Here we must use some skill,' began my leader, 'in clinging, now here, now there, to the wall that recedes.' And this made our steps so slow that the waning moon reached her bed, to lie down again, before we were out of that needle's eye. But when at last we were free in the open, above, where the mountainside draws back, — I weary, and both of us doubtful about our way, — we stopped on a flat place, more solitary than roads through deserts. From the edge that borders the void to the foot of the high bank, which goes straight up, is perhaps three times the length of a human body; and as far as my sight could fly, first to the left side, then to the right, this shelf looked to me just the same."

Higher up on the mountain the travelers are enveloped in a thick cloud of smoke, which calls up the picture of Alpine mists: "Remember, reader, — if ever in the Alps a fog has caught thee, through which thou couldst see no better than a mole sees through its filmy eye, — remember how, when the thick, wet vapors begin to grow thinner, the disk of the sun feebly shows through them, and thy fancy will quickly come to see how I first beheld the sun again, just as it was on the point of setting."

Down on the damp, breezy shore, the rushes grow, close to the sea: "This little isle, round about its lowest edge, down yonder where the waves plash, bears rushes on the soft ooze. No other plant, that puts forth leaves or hardens, can live there, because it yields not to the gusts." There it is that the dew is slowest to evaporate: "We were walking over the lonely flatland, like one who is going back to his lost path, and, until he reaches it, thinks he is moving to no purpose. When we had come to a spot where the dew contends with the sunshine, and, being in a cool place, is little rarified, my master gently laid both his hands, wide open, on the grass."

In the following description of a waterfall, we find once more a specific locality: " I was following him; and we had gone but a little way when the noise of the water was so close that, had we spoken, we could scarcely have heard each other. Even as the first river that has a course of its own to the east from Monviso, on the left slope of the Apennines (called Acquacheta above, before coming down into its low bed, but bereft of that name at Forlì), even as this river reverberates there above St. Benedict's in the Alps, — because it shoots down a single fall instead of being divided into a thousand, — thus, falling over a precipitous bank, we found that dark water reëchoing so loud that in a little while it would have hurt the ear."

Effective use is made by Dante, in Purgatory, of his shadow, which differentiates him from the disembodied inhabitants and also from Virgil, his companion. In Hell it was too dark for the souls to see whether he cast a shadow or not; but in Purgatory, in the daytime, his opaqueness cannot escape notice. First of all, Dante himself is startled, — at sunrise, as he and his master are standing side by side, with their backs to the east, — to see only one shadow cast before them: " The light of the sun, which was flaming ruddy behind us, was broken, in front of me, in the shape which the stoppage of its rays found in me. I turned to one side, fearing I was forsaken, when I saw the earth darkened in front of me alone. And my comforter said: 'Why art thou distrustful?' Here he turned quite around towards me: 'Dost thou not believe that I am with thee, guiding thee?'"

Presently the souls on the mountainside take notice of Dante's shade: "I had already left these ghosts, and was following my leader's footprints, when one of them shouted behind me, lifting up his finger: 'Look! the sunbeam does not seem to shine on the left of that lower figure, and he seems to act like a living man!' I turned my eyes, at the sound of this speech, and saw them staring in amazement at me, at me alone, and at the broken light. 'Why,' said my master, 'is thy mind so caught that thou slackenest thy gait? What matters it to thee what they whisper here?' . . . Meanwhile across the slope, a little ahead of us, a crowd was singing *Miserere* in alternation. When they saw that I, with my body, did not give way to the passage of the rays, they changed their song into a long, hoarse 'Oh!' And two of them, after the fashion of messengers, ran to meet us, and questioned us. 'Let us know what ye are!'"

As Dante walks along the outer edge of the path, on the brink of the cliff, to keep clear of a mass of fire that juts out over most of the way, his shadow, falling on the yellow flame, turns it red; and a crowd of souls, marching in the blaze, observe his presence by this change of color: "While we were proceeding thus along the rim,

one by one, and my kind master kept saying,
'Take heed, mind my warning,' the sun was shining on my right shoulder, for already its radiance
was turning all the west from azure to white; and
I was making the flame look ruddier with my
shadow, and even at that slight hint I saw many
spirits take notice, as they went by. Thus it was
that they began to speak of me; for they went on
to say to one another: 'This one does not look
like an unsubstantial body.' Then some came
towards me, as far as they could, always careful
not to come out where they should not burn."

Once again the living Dante is an object of
amazement — this time, in the circle of gluttony:
"Our speech did not delay our going, nor our
going our speech; but, conversing, we went briskly
on, like a ship pushed by a fair wind. And the
souls, which looked like things twice dead, observing that I was alive, sucked in wonder of me
through their hollow eyes."

These scattered passages show how skilfully
the poet could ring changes on one theme. Let
us turn to another. In the following lines, it is
three in the afternoon, and Dante, as he walks,
is just facing the sunset; "and the sunbeams
struck the middle of our noses (because we had
so encircled the mountain that we were walking straight toward the setting sun), when, all
at once, I felt my brow much more weighed down
with brightness than it had been before, and, not
knowing why, I was amazed." First he tries,
with his hands, to shade his eyes from this in-

creased light, but in vain; then he conjectures that it may be refracted upward by some pool in his path; finally he asks Virgil: "'What is it, sweet father, from which I cannot screen my eyes enough to help me, and which seems to be moving towards us?' 'Marvel not,' he answered, 'if the family of Heaven still dazzles thee. It is a messenger arrived to bid us mount. Soon it shall come to pass that the sight of such things shall not be a pain, but a gladness as great as nature has prepared thee to enjoy.'"

With angels, we pass beyond the field of experience into the realm of creative imagination.

> Came forth the lovely creature from afar,
> Its raiment white, as beautiful its head
> As looks to us the twinkling morning star.
> It spread its arms, and then its wings it spread.
> "O come, draw near, the stairs are close at hand,
> And all the climb is easy now," it said.

Of course, angels had in art already assumed a certain conventional exterior; but of that Dante really keeps only the sublimated human form and the wings. His angelic figures are made up almost wholly of sweetness and light. One of them speaks "in a voice far more living than ours." It is the function of another of these heavenly messengers to transport souls in a boat from the Tiber's mouth to the island of Purgatory. The souls in question belong to Christians who have just died penitent; and the Tiber's mouth represents the bosom of the Church. Dante and Virgil are on the shore of the island, newly ar-

rived, when they see, in the distance, first the
angel's shining face, then its white wings and garment, finally the craft. "We were still close to
the sea, like people wondering about their way,
heart pressing forward, body standing motionless,
when lo! — even as Mars, at the approach of
morn, shines red through the thick mist, down in
the west, just above the ocean level, — so there
appeared to me (as I hope to see it again!) a
light coming over the water so swift that no flight
can compare with its speed. And when I had for
a moment withdrawn my eye from it, to question
my leader, I saw it again, bigger and brighter.
Next, on either side of it, something white appeared, and beneath, little by little, another white-
ness. My master as yet spake not a word, until
the first white spots revealed themselves as wings.
As soon as he was sure who the boatman was, he
shouted: 'Down, down on thy knees! Here is
God's angel! Clasp thy hands! Henceforth thou
shalt meet such ministers as these. See how he
scorns all human instruments, plying no oar, nor
other sail than his own wings, between such distant shores. See how he holds his pinions uplifted
toward heaven, fanning the air with those eternal
plumes, which change not like the hair of mortals.'
Then, as the bird of God came nearer and nearer,
it shone brighter still, so bright that my eye could
not endure it close at hand; and I looked down.
The angel came ashore with a little boat so light
that the water swallowed none of it. At the stern
stood the heavenly helmsman, — such a shape

that the mere description of it would be a bene-
diction, — and within sat more than a hundred
spirits, all of them singing together, with one
voice, ' When Israel went out of Egypt,' and the
rest of the psalm that follows in the writ. Then
he made over them the sign of the holy cross,
whereat they all threw themselves on the shore;
and he departed, fleet as he had come."

Here is a scene, just as original in its conception,
but as different in character as picture can be from
picture. We are in the very core of the earth,
beside Satan — a vast monstrous form, wedged
into a mass of rock and ice, his upper part projecting into Hell, his legs into a cave on the other
side. Now, near his middle is the centre of our
globe, the centre of gravity of all matter: Satan's
head, therefore, is *above* the middle on one side
of that centre; but his feet are *above* it on the
other. For a straight *downward* motion, if it be
continued in the same direction beyond the earth's
centre, becomes an *upward* motion as soon as it
crosses that point. Dante and Virgil have pursued
such a course: they have crawled through a crack,
passed the middle point of the globe, and emerged
into a cavern still very close to the centre, but belonging to the other hemisphere. Dante as yet
does not realize what they have done, having been
carried on Virgil's back.

> From out the crevice of a stone he crept,
>   And on the nearest edge he seated me,
>   Then cautiously across to me he stept.
> I lifted up my eyes, and thought to see

VISION

The shape of Satan we had left behind,
But saw, projecting upward, shank and knee.
Now let the reader ignorant and blind,
Who doth not understand what we had past,
Imagine how distracted was my mind.

Solid realism is the tone of Dante's Hell; his Purgatory is still of earth, but surrounded by a celestial atmosphere; his Heaven is compounded almost exclusively of light and music. Think, then, what almost superhuman resourcefulness is required to diversify the stages of his journey through the skies! In one place, dancing rings of bright spirits; in another, a ladder of light, extending beyond the range of vision, with souls flitting over it; in still another, a vast army of militant ghosts collected in the form of a gigantic fiery cross, like two Milky Ways intersecting at right angles, and all alive with song. Elsewhere a host of shining souls takes the form of an Eagle, symbol of the Holy Roman Empire, which flaps its wings like a real bird, and speaks with a single voice.

Methought I heard a river murmuring
Adown its clear descent from stone to stone,
A witness to its bounteous mountain spring.
As music in the zither takes its tone
Along the neck, and in the tuneful reed
Along the holes wherein the breath is blown,
Thus, rising up with never-changing speed,
Within the eagle flowed a murmuring thrill
Along the neck, as 't were a hollow weed;
There turned to voice, and issued thro' the bill,
Pronouncing words, which my expectant heart,
That wrote them down, with exstasy did fill.

THE POWER OF DANTE

Dante's first experience of heaven is his rapid
ascent, with Beatrice, from the Garden of Eden to
the moon, into whose substance they penetrate.

The inborn thirst for Heaven, which never dies,
　　Was sweeping us along from where we were,
　　Wellnigh as swift as turn the wheeling skies.
My lady lookt aloft, and I at her;
　　And quicker than a bolt can fly and light
　　And quit the notch, with nothing to deter,
I saw myself transported to a site
　　Where something wonderful mine eyes did meet.
　　And she who readeth all my thoughts aright
Now turned to me as glad as she was sweet:
　　"Thank God within thy heart," she said, "who thus
　　Hath carried us his lowest star to greet."
Methought a heavy cloud envelopt us,
　　Solid but gleaming, limpid yet opaque,
　　Like diamond made by sunshine luminous.
Inside itself th' eternal pearl did take
　　Both her and me, as water takes a ray
　　Of sunlight piercing thro' without a break.

Now Beatrice, with her disciple, is about to
flash from the moon to the planet Mercury, and
stands gazing up toward the Empyrean:

My lady spake as I to write contrive;
　　Then turned, all full of yearning wistfulness,
　　Toward the quarter that is most alive.
Her changing form and silence motionless
　　Restrain my eager mind, which speaketh not,
　　Tho' questions new and strange begin to press.
Like arrowhead that hits the target's dot
　　Before the quivering string hath come to rest,
　　So we into the second kingdom shot.
Such happiness my lady there possest

That, when she stopt within the planet bright,
That orb with greater brilliancy was blest.
And if the smiling star increast its light,
  Then what became of me, whose natural mood
  Is sensitive to every sound and sight?
As in a limpid pond the finny brood
  Come swimming up, when falleth from above
  A thing that hath to them the look of food,
So I beheld a thousand splendors move,
  Approaching us, and each appeared to cry:
  "Lo! here is one who shall increase our love!"

In this conception of things never seen by mortal eye, Dante goes beyond the usual domain of poets; but he passes even further. The pictures thus far drawn, though novel in their totality, are made of materials known to the senses. But in his figures of celestial joy, his "smile of the universe," in his symbols of Grace and of God, he transcends the bounds of description, conveying, through means necessarily finite and material, the impression of immaterial infinity. This is suggestion, not painting. It is "such stuff as dreams are made on"—dreams, which faintly linger when we first awake, and which we afterwards vainly struggle to recall.

So slumber breaks, when smites the covered eye
  A new and suddenly appearing light;
  And, breaking, quivers ere it wholly die.
        .   .   .
A man was I who dimly catches sight
  Of some forgotten dream, and tries and tries
  To bring it back to mind, but cannot quite.

One more dream-passage I shall cite in conclusion. It tells what Dante experienced in endeavoring to reduce to words his ineffable concept; it tells what we, on closing the *Paradise,* think we have felt.

> E'en as a man who seeth in his sleep,
>   Whose mood still lingers, when the dream is done,
>   Tho' nothing else the memory can keep,
> E'en so am I; for what my sleep hath spun
>   Is almost wholly gone, yet still doth ease
>   My heart a sweetness from the vision won.
> Thus snow, unlockt by sunshine, swiftly flees;
>   Thus Sybil's wisdom, writ on fluttering leaves,
>   Was wafted off forever by the breeze.

LECTURE VI

CONCEPTION

At the close of the *Vita Nuova* — that wonderfully discreet record of Dante's emotional life under the influence of Beatrice — a strange, fascinating, baffling combination of self-revelation and reticence — we find a sonnet which tells how the poet's thought, in the form of a sigh, soars through all the revolving skies, and, piercing the outermost and greatest, leaving the world of matter behind, enters Paradise, where it beholds the soul of Beatrice in glory.

> Beyond the sphere that all-encircling sways
>   A sigh, escaping from my heart, doth fare.
>   An insight new, which Love, so full of care,
> Inspireth now, impels it up always.
> When it has reacht the goal for which it prays,
>   It sees a lady full of honor there;
>   And on her light, which shines beyond compare,
> The pilgrim spirit wondering doth gaze.
> 'T is all so strange that, when it tells me this,
>   I cannot comprehend, it puzzles so
>   The mournful heart which ever bids it tell.
>   It speaketh of that gentle one, I know,
> Because it often nameth Beatrice;
>   And that, dear ladies mine, I hear full well.

"After this sonnet," continues Dante, "there appeared to me a marvelous vision, wherein I saw

[155]

things that made me determine to say no more of this blessed one until I should be able to speak of her more fitly. And to that end am I studying with all my strength, as she verily knoweth. Wherefore, if it shall be the pleasure of Him through whom all things live that my life be prolonged some years, I hope to say of her what never yet was said of woman. And then may He, who is the Lord of kindness, grant that my soul go forth to behold the glory of its lady, of that blessed Beatrice, who doth gloriously behold the face of Him who is blessed forever."

A hope and a prayer that were surely both fulfilled! A monument such as never before — nor since — was erected to any woman, he verily builded; and, if we may believe the testimony of those nearest him, his soul went forth just after the completion of his great task. When he wrote the lines I have quoted, he was some twenty-eight or twenty-nine years old, midway in his earthly career, for he died at the age of fifty-six. Many cares, labors, and trials intervened; but during a great part of this second half of his life he must have carried his mighty project in mind. Vast preparatory studies are foreshadowed in the passage cited; and much of the knowledge he thereby acquired was eventually set forth in other works — principally in the *Banquet* and in the treatise *On Vernacular Composition*. Both of these, however, he left unfinished, and returned to his first design.

Now, what was the monument to Beatrice, as

he conceived it? What was the "marvelous vision" that flashed upon him, "after this sonnet?" What conception should we expect of a man of his faith, his ethical standards, his character, his experience, his poetic genius — and, let us not forget to add, his time? The sonnet itself and the following prose reveal something of his idea: his tribute was to be a vision of Heaven, with Beatrice there enthroned, whatever else it might come to convey. We may infer also that it was to picture her as the guiding spirit of his own progress heavenward, as, indeed, she is already sketched in the *Vita Nuova*. If so, there must have been the purpose of a mystic journey, like that of Bunyan's Christian. We have, then, thus far, the conception of an ascent of Dante's soul, led by his lady, from the sin and sorrow of earth to the pure joy of Paradise, where Beatrice dwells in glory. But such a narrative is really a spiritual autobiography, a sequel to the tale told in the *New Life,* though related on a grander scale. As it grows, as it deepens, the poet's experience becomes typical of the history of all mankind.

Such an undertaking indeed demands faith, moral insight, character, acquaintance with the world, poetic imagination. The need of these attributes is self-evident; but why should it call for extensive preliminary study on the part of the writer? Perhaps to round out his theology and ethics, to increase through books his knowledge of man, and to improve his literary form by copy of the best examples. Without doubt these objects

were in the author's mind; but I think there was
something more. Dante was eager to help his
fellowmen, and to help them in more ways than
one. Utility his book would not lack, if it pointed
the way to Heaven; but man wants guidance likewise for his earthly walks, and good teaching was
scarce. The monumental poem was to be also a
storehouse of information, a banquet of philosophy. " The great unspeakable Providence," says
Dante in his *Monarchy*, "hath set two ends for
the pursuit of man: to wit, the happiness of this
life . . . and the happiness of life eternal. . . .
And to these happinesses, as to different goals, we
must come by different means. For to the first
we come by philosophical teachings, if we follow
them, acting in accordance with the moral and
intellectual virtues. But to the second, by spiritual
teachings, which transcend human reason, if we
follow them, acting in accordance with the theological virtues, Faith, Hope, and Love."

The great poem over which the spirit of Beatrice was to preside, was destined, then, to be a
guide to both heavenly and earthly happiness. In
form, it was to be the story of Dante's own salvation; his passage from sin to repentance, and
through reason and discipline to purity; from
worldly cares to contemplation of the divine. The
tale is told in the first person: it is unmistakably
Dante's own; to stamp its authenticity beyond
mistake, he introduces, at the middle stage of his
progress, his name — which, he declares, " is
bound to be registered here." Now, in general,'

the author believed that it is unbecoming to speak of one's self, because one cannot do so without praising or blaming, both of which are undignified. There are, however, certain circumstances under which such speech is legitimate. After an unjust accusation, it is lawful to discuss one's self to prove one's innocence. Also it is right to do so, "when," as Dante says in his *Banquet,* "by speaking of one's self very great help is given to others, in the way of teaching; and this consideration moved St. Augustine, in his *Confessions,* to talk about himself; for by the course of his life, which was from evil to good, from good to better, and from better to best, he offered an example and a lesson such as could be received from no other witness so trustworthy as he."

For the autobiographical side of his poem, Dante found, therefore, a precedent, and, in a very general sense, a model, in the *Confessions* of St. Augustine. For the fiction of a vision of the other world, he had as inspiration, on the one hand, the sixth book of the *Æneid,* which relates the descent of Æneas into the world of the dead, and, on the other, a mass of medieval legend — the Irish stories of Tundal and of St. Patrick's Purgatory, the vision of the Italian Friar Alberic, and, oldest of the lot, the so-called Apocalypse of St. Paul. This last was a Greek document of the end of the fourth century, narrating the journey of St. Paul, guided by an angel, through Hell, Purgatory, and Heaven; though never accepted by the Church, it became, in Latin and vernacular translations, immensely popular. Now, while Dante adopted none of these works as a pattern, he knew them; they were in his consciousness when he planned his monument, the character of which they helped to determine. There must have been also in his store of recollections some stories of marvelous journeys, such as that of the Irish monk, St. Brendan, who sailed afar out into the Atlantic and discovered the Isle of the Blest; or that of three Eastern monks, who, following up a stream, climbed a mountain a hundred miles high, on whose summit they found the Garden of Eden; or, hardly less wonderful, the real travels of Marco Polo in Asia. Here, too, there is no question of imitation (save perhaps a stray detail here and there); there is nothing more than a general coloring of Dante's imagination. For the idea of a great granary of wisdom, suggestion was ready at hand in the ancient and the medieval encyclopedias, whose compilers strove to collect and transmit in convenient form the accumulated knowledge of foregoing generations of scholars. Such a compendium was the *Treasure* of Dante's elderly friend and counselor, Brunetto Latini.

This same Florentine, Master Brunetto, wrote, however, something vastly more important for the genesis of the conception of the *Divine Comedy* — the *Tesoretto,* or *Little Treasure,* which really combines in itself nearly all the elements I have enumerated: it is a confession, a fantastic journey, a compilation of learning, and it may perhaps be called a vision. Furthermore,

CONCEPTION

it is cast in allegorical form, and in verse — poor
enough verse, to be sure, mere doggerel couplets:
still, a poem, an allegorical poem, relating a quest
for happiness, told in the first person.   Here we
have, no doubt, the most important single suggestion among those which contributed to the plan
of the *Divine Comedy*.   The two works are as
far apart as two poems well can be, and Dante's
reminiscences of the *Little Treasure* are so petty
that scarcely anyone has thought it worth while
to mention them; yet to Brunetto Latini he owed
a debt in which all lovers of the *Divina Commedia* have a share — a debt which Dante himself
fully appreciated.   The soul of Master Brunetto,
encountered in the world below, speaks to him
these words:

> If but thy star shall guide thee with its light,
>   A glorious haven shalt thou surely see,
>   If in the happy life I judged aright.
> If death had not so promptly taken me,
>   Knowing that Heaven to thee had been so kind,
>   In thine emprise I should have heartened thee.

And the poet replies:

> If favoring Heaven upon my wishes smiled,
>   If God my whole entreaty would allow,
>   You were not yet from human life exiled.
> For stampt upon my mind (a sadness now)
>   Your friendly, dear, paternal face I see,
>   As in the world you ever taught me how
> A mortal man may win eternity.
>   How deep my gratitude, in all my speech,
>   As long as I shall live, revealed must be.

I have said that Brunetto's *Little Treasure* is an allegory; it begins, however, with a bit of historical fact. Here is its story, in a few words. Returning in 1260 from Spain, whither he had (in reality) been sent by Florence on a mission to Alfonso X of Castile, he hears on the way the news of the battle of Montaperti and the bloody defeat of the Guelfs. In sad meditation over this disaster to his party, he loses his way in a strange wood. Suddenly he comes to his senses, and sees near by the beautiful and majestic figure of a lady, Dame Nature, who imparts to him a great deal of erudition. Then he travels through a wilderness, until he reaches a lovely plain, the land of Virtue, inhabited by emperors, kings, and scholars, governed by the four Cardinal Virtues (whose palaces he inspects), with Virtue — unqualified — as Empress over all. Yet this does not satisfy him, for he craves love and joy. Resuming his journey, he finds at last the country he has sought, the land of Love — a fascinating and mysterious region. In a flowery meadow, which is forever changing, are throngs of people, some gay, some sad; and in their midst sits enthroned a winged youth named Pleasure, who is constantly shooting arrows into the crowd. Here, as in the land of Virtue, there are four queens: Fear, Longing, Love, Hope. The poet, after having been instructed in the theory of love, falls under the dominion of that passion. From this dangerous predicament he is saved by Ovid — who, in the Middle Ages, was regarded as a moralist, his work being interpreted allegorically. Through suitable penance, Brunetto attains purity. Renouncing the quest of worldly happiness, he returns to the wood, hoping to find the way to the land of the Seven Liberal Arts, the land of Learning. Many countries are traversed. Persistently he rides on until he scales Olympus, on whose summit he encounters a venerable white-bearded figure. This is Ptolemy, master of astronomy and philosophy, whom the traveler eagerly questions. We are now prepared for a feast of reason; but at this point the poem breaks off. This symbolic moral narrative — with its strange wood, its search for true happiness, its introduction of a Latin poet as a rescuer, its didactic female figure of Dame Nature, its ascent of a lofty mountain, its reverend sage at the close — contains the suggestion for much of the framework of the *Commedia*.

The main scenery of Dante's poem may be found, in germ, in the *Vision of St. Paul* and the legends that followed it, telling of visits to the other world; in the *Æneid;* and in stories of the Earthly Paradise. Its real theme, the experience of a human soul snatched from perdition to the way of salvation, was probably inspired, if it had any external source, by St. Augustine's *Confessions*. There remains the rôle of Beatrice, in whose honor the *Divine Comedy* was first designed. Her figure in the great poem has, to be sure, something in common with Brunetto's Dame Nature; but it has much closer kinship with the

Lady Philosophy who comes to comfort Boëthius in his prison and expounds to him the teachings of the Greek thinkers. The *Consolation of Philosophy,* by Boëthius (a late Latin statesman, scholar, philosopher, and literary artist), was the first book of secular philosophy studied by Dante, who had recourse to it in his desolation after the death of Beatrice.

We have collected the materials — very good materials, too, although only one man has ever lived who could have built of them the greatest of all poems. The truth is, of course, that Dante did not really construct with the materials furnished him: what he derived from his sources shrinks into insignificance when compared to what he drew from his own experience and his own imagination. Even in outward shaping he is amazingly original. His work displays in the highest degree a fundamental structural quality that is quite lacking in his predecessors, and is, indeed, but little exemplified by the other world-masterpieces of all ages. I mean symmetry. The *Iliad* perhaps comes nearest to the *Divine Comedy* in this respect; but still how far removed! Next one might name Chaucer's *Canterbury Tales.* The *Odyssey,* the *Æneid, Paradise Lost* show but vague outlines. Goethe's *Faust,* virtually none at all.

One cannot read very far in Dante without observing how dear to him is this quality of symmetry; how clear is the evidence, in his works, of a distinct architectural bent. Our poet was at one time appointed in Florence a commissioner to superintend the alteration of a street; but whether or not this charge implies a recognition of architectural study or talent, it would be rash to guess. We know that he could draw; for in the *Vita Nuova* he speaks of designing figures of angels on the anniversary of his lady's death; and in the *Divina Commedia* there is at least one simile that could scarcely have occurred to a man unfamiliar with the technical difficulties of painting. " Men call a thing beautiful," says Dante in the *Banquet,* " when its parts properly correspond in such a way that their harmony gives pleasure. Hence a man appears handsome when his limbs are in proper proportion; and we call a song beautiful when the words that compose it are in harmony with one another, according to the demands of the art. Therefore is that discourse most beautiful whose parts most suitably harmonize." In his treatise on vernacular poetry he defines the *canzone,* or ode, as the elegant combination of equal stanzas, without a refrain, into a single theme; and he announces his intention of proving in the third part of this work (which unfortunately was never written) that the ode is " something sublime."

Several of Dante's lyrics show a predilection for groupings based on the number three. He was, in general, much addicted to arranging things in threes or multiples of three. One *canzone* is written in three languages: Provençal, Latin, and Italian. His Latin treatise on *Monarchy* is in three books: the first arguing that mankind needs one general government, superior to all local rule; the second, that the Roman Empire was predestined to fill this need; the third, that the Emperor derives his authority from God directly, and is not subordinate to the Pope. Dante's principal Italian works form a great trilogy, the *New Life,* the *Banquet,* the *Divine Comedy.* The *New Life* itself has as its nucleus a group of three odes.

If we look more closely at the architecture of this "little book," we shall discern a curiously patterned framework. As you know, the *Vita Nuova* consists of a series of poems, selected by Dante in 1293 or '94 from his previous work, and arranged presumably in chronological order; with a prose explanation that forms a more or less consecutive story, the poems being embedded, at intervals, in the prose. Now, these poems are in number thirty-one, three of them being long *canzoni,* while twenty-eight are shorter compositions. The twenty-eight lesser ones are all sonnets, except three: one of these is a ballad; one is a stanza of an interrupted *canzone;* the third is called by the author a *canzone,* but, having only two stanzas, is rather of the type known in Provence as a half-*canzone.* It seems, then, legitimate to group all these twenty-eight briefer poems together, as contrasted with the three long odes, or full *canzoni.* If we do so, we find that the poems of the *Vita Nuova* are arranged in a regular scheme: in the centre, three odes, the middle one being separated from each of the others by four short pieces; before the three odes, ten short pieces; after the three, ten short pieces. In other words, the order of little and big is this: ten, *one,* four, *one,* four, *one,* ten. But there is another division, according to the subject-matter — a division into three parts, almost exactly equal in length, but not marked in any obvious way by the author. Part One comprises the period between Dante's first sight of Beatrice and his conversion to platonic love; Part Two, the period between this conversion and the death of his lady; Part Three, the period between her passing and his vision of her in Paradise. The work begins, therefore, with her first appearance to him on earth, and ends with her first appearance to him in Heaven. The two symmetries, of form and of substance, are quite independent of each other. Both are so unobtrusive that a reader may study the book attentively, many times, without observing either. The *New Life* would seem to be thus conceived rather for the satisfaction of an inner craving than for the sake of producing an effect on its audience.

Very conspicuous, on the contrary, in the same work, is a multiple of three, the number nine, which accompanies Beatrice in her relations with Dante. The ninth hour is especially persistent. After his lady's death, the author offers an explanation of the mysterious affinity between her and the recurrent nine. She died, as we make out from the somewhat cryptic text, early in the evening of June 8, 1290. This date containing but one nine, Dante, in order to bring in the mystic number three times, has recourse to the calendars of Araby and Syria, about which his textbook of astronomy offered him some information. The Syrians begin their year with October, so that June is their ninth month. The Arabs, beginning their day with sunset, regard the close of our June 8 as the first part of their June 9. Thus we get three nines, in the day, the month, and the year. Now let us hear what Dante himself says:—

" I declare that according to the usage of Araby her most noble soul departed in the first hour of the ninth day of the month; and according to the usage of Syria she departed in the ninth month of the year, for the first month there is Tisrin First, which is our October. And according to our usage she departed in that year of our indiction (that is, of the years of our Lord) in which the perfect number [ten] was nine times completed in that century in which she was placed in this world; and she was one of the Christians of the thirteenth century [she died in the year 90 of the thirteenth century of the Christian era]. Why this number was so friendly to her, the following might be a reason: forasmuch as, according to Ptolemy and according to Christian truth, nine are the heavens that move, and, according to common astrological opinion, the aforesaid heavens operate here below in accordance with their relation to one another, this number was friendly to her to show that in her generation all nine moving heavens were in perfect harmony together. This is one reason

for it; but, considering more subtly and in accordance with infallible truth, this number was she
herself — I mean figuratively, and I understand
it thus: the number three is the root of nine, because, without any other number, by itself it makes
nine; as we plainly see that three times three is
nine.   Therefore if three is by itself the maker
of nine, and the Maker of miracles by himself is
three (to wit, Father, Son, and Holy Ghost, which
are three and one) this lady was accompanied by
the number nine to show that she was a nine, that
is, a miracle, whose root is the wondrous Trinity
alone.   Perhaps by a subtler person could be found
in this a still subtler reason; but this is the one
that I see and like best."

Three is the symbol of the Godhead; and nine,
or what three makes of itself, is the symbol of a
miracle, which God makes of himself: therefore
nine is the number that befits the miraculous
Beatrice.   Such is Dante's complicated argument.
It must be remembered that in the Middle Ages
the symbolism of numbers formed a recognized
branch of philosophical inquiry.   The subject is
discussed at length by such masters as St. Augustine, Rabanus Maurus, Hugh of St. Victor.   An
inevitable significance is imposed on certain numbers by association with Christian theology.   The
most important of these is *three*, — the favorite
number, also, in folk-lore and in general popular
use.

On *three* is based the whole plan of the *Divine
Comedy*.   In the first place, the entire poem is
composed in *terza rima,* a sequence of groups of

three lines, the second line of each group riming with the first and third of the next. In the second place, the *Commedia* consists of three parts, *Inferno, Purgatorio, Paradiso*. These are divided into cantos (that is, in Italian, *canti,* or " songs "), of unequal length, but on the average, of about one hundred and forty lines each. The whole work contains just a hundred cantos — the " perfect number " multiplied by itself. The first canto being, however, a sort of introduction to all the poem, there remain ninety-nine cantos, which are evenly distributed among the three parts, each receiving thirty-three.

So much for the external form. In the matter of the *Commedia* we observe the same prominence of the " mystic number." There are three realms of the dead. Hell is composed of three parts, where are punished respectively sins of weakness, violence, and fraud. The mountain on the solitary island is also tripartite, consisting of Purgatory itself, of the slopes below it, and of the Garden of Eden above it. Heaven likewise may be separated into three regions: first the spheres within the reach of the earth's shadow (those of the moon, Mercury, and Venus) ; second, those beyond the shadow but below the fixed stars (the spheres of the sun, Mars, Jupiter, and Saturn) ; third, the sky of the fixed stars, the invisible outermost crystalline heaven, and the Empyrean or true Paradise of spirit.

Coming to the narrative itself, we encounter the same number. Three beasts — a leopard, a

lion, and a wolf — block Dante's passage up the
Delectable Mountain; but he is rescued by three
ladies who care for him in Heaven: the Virgin
Mary, St. Lucia, and Beatrice. Dante spends
three nights, and has three allegorical dreams, on
the mountain of Purgatory. Even in little details
the same predilection is evident. The bank which
the poet descends to reach the Valley of the
Princes, on the slope of the mountain, is three
steps deep; the stream that separates him from
Matilda, in the Garden of Eden, is three steps
broad. Three stairs — perhaps representing original innocence, sin, and atonement — lead to the
gate of Purgatory. Satan has three faces. St.
Peter encircles Dante three times, in token of his
satisfaction over the poet's successful examination
in Faith. Three times Virgil calls Dante, to
arouse him from his stupor, after one of his
visions. Three times does Dante try to embrace
the intangible shade of the musician, Casella,
which he meets on the island of Purgatory.

> One of the souls, I saw, advancing came
>   To clasp me in its arms, so lovingly
>   I felt a keen desire to do the same.
> O shadows vain to touch, tho' plain to see!
>   Three times behind it I my hands did hook;
>   Three times I brought them empty back to me.
> My face, I think, assumed a wondering look;
>   Whereat the shadow smiled and drew away.
>   Pursuing it, a forward step I took.
> Right gently, then, it counseled me to stay.
>   At that I recognized it, and besought
>   The shade to stop, a word with me to say.

One is surprised that Dante, with his love of symmetry and his fondness for three, should not have provided himself with a separate guide for each of the three kingdoms he has to traverse. As it is, Virgil conducts him through Hell and Purgatory, Beatrice through Heaven. In the latter part of the second realm, to be sure, Statius is added to the two companions, and explains some things which are perhaps a little beyond the reach of the pagan Virgil; for Dante chose to regard Statius as having been on earth a Christian, secretly converted. Now, it may be, of course, that in his first conception, the poet planned to make Statius the guide throughout Purgatory, in which case there would have been an exact harmony in the three parts of the poem. But if he ever had such a design, he abandoned it; perhaps because he could not make it fit his allegory, perhaps because he had become so fond of Virgil that he was loath to give him up. For Virgil, symbolic though he was, had become very real to Dante. The directing personages of the *Divine Comedy* are both real and allegorical: Virgil is Reason, Cato of Utica is Free Will, Beatrice is Revelation, St. Bernard is Intuition; but they are still Virgil, Cato, Beatrice, and St. Bernard.

That Dante's monumental poem should be allegorically conceived was inevitable. His whole philosophy was steeped in symbolism, and allegory was in his day regarded as the highest type of literary composition. From the early centuries of Christianity the Bible had been expounded allegorically; symbolism pervaded religious service and religious architecture. Moreover, the same method of interpretation had been applied to the myths of Homer; Virgil and Ovid were looked upon as master allegorists; and we have reason to believe that Dante found Christian allegory in Statius. In French, the most fashionable poem was the allegorical *Romance of the Rose;* in Italian, Dante had before him the *Little Treasure* of his friendly adviser. Even in his own *New Life,* the God of Love may be called an allegorical figure. Between the *Vita Nuova* and the *Divina Commedia,* we find in his work two allegories, one of them continued through several poems, the other confined to a single ode. As the latter is the shorter and the less known, let us consider it first.

The *canzone* in question, *Tre donne intorno al cor mi son venute,* is a poem of exile. Carducci thought it the noblest of Dante's allegorical lyrics. It begins thus:

Three ladies round my heart are clustering,
 And seat themselves outside.
 Within doth Love reside,
Who hath my whole existence in his care.
So fair and good are they, the mighty king
 (I mean the trusty guide
 Who in my heart doth bide)
To speak of their distress can hardly bear.
Mournful appears each one, and in despair,
A weary creature, into exile hurled,
Forsaken by the world,
 Whose virtue and estate are no defence.
 In times not distant hence

Men showed them love, they say; now they are shown
Nothing but hate and cold indifference.
These ladies all alone
Have come to seek a home, knowing full well
My heart contains the friend of whom I tell.

One lady, — who leans her head on her hand like
a plucked rose, and whose tears drip on her bare
arm, while the other hand hides her weeping face,
— is questioned by Love, indignant at her poverty
and her shameful rags. And she replies, sighing:
" O food of few, it is our divine kinship that sends
us to thee. I, the saddest, am thy mother's sister.
I am Justice, tattered as thou seest." [Love, or
Cupid, was the son of Venus; and Venus and
Astræa, the goddess of Justice, were both daugh-
ters of Jupiter.] When she had thus made herself known, grief and shame seized my lord, and
he asked who were the other two that were with
her. And she that was so prone to tears, fired with
fresh grief at his words, replied: " As thou must
know, the Nile rises as a tiny stream from a spring
[in the Garden of Eden]. There, where the foliage of the osier shades the earth from the great
sunshine, above the virgin waters, I bore her who
is at my side, wiping her eyes with her blond
tresses. This beauteous offspring of mine, gazing
at herself in the clear spring, conceived the third,
who is furthest from me." [Who are these mysterious ladies — mother, daughter, and grand-
daughter, the first a goddess, the other two
immaculately born in the Earthly Paradise?
Dante's son Pietro, in his commentary on the

[174]

Divine Comedy, refers to them, and states that his father intended them to signify Divine Right, Human Right (born of Divine Right in the first abode of man), and Law (the reflection of Human Right, assuming a form as soon as mankind came into existence). This interpretation, which meets all the requirements of the text, is probably correct. Divine Right, Human Right, and Law appear as exiles to Dante, an outcast himself, just as to St. Francis there once appeared (according to St. Bonaventure) the three ladies, Poverty, Chastity, and Obedience. There exists, unpublished, a long commentary on this poem, written about 1400, which is said to be worthless in most respects, but which affords one bit of information that may be true — namely, that the ode was written in 1311, when Florence granted amnesty to many of her banished citizens, but not to Dante. That the author was an exile at the time of writing, is made evident by the poem itself. Let us see how it continues.] Sighs at first prevent Love from speaking. After a little, his once wayward eyes wet with tears, he greets his disconsolate kinswomen. Then, picking up his arrows [one of gold, one of lead, as Ovid describes them], he says: "Lift up your heads! Here are the weapons I once chose; they are tarnished from disuse. Bounty and Temperance and the other ladies born of our blood now go a-begging. Yet if this be grievous, it is for the eyes and lips of men to bewail it, unhappy men, whose star has consigned them to this age; not for us, who belong to the

eternal citadel. If we are now wounded, we shall
not always be; for a race shall return which shall
make this arrow bright again." [The last full
stanza I shall attempt to render metrically, as I
did the first:]

>And I, who hear exiles as grand as these
>   Take comfort, then repine,
>   With eloquence divine,
>Am prone to glory in my banishment.
>For if the power of destiny decrees
>   That in this world malign
>   White flowers to black decline,
>To fall among the good is heaven-sent.
>And 'neath my burden I could be content,
>If only I were not so far removed
>From what my eyes have loved,
>   Whose loss hath lit a burning fire in me,
>   Which hath so utterly
>   Consumed the flesh and bones I dwelt within
>That Death against my breast hath set his key.
>   Wherefore, if I did sin,
>My fault is dead and gone, this many a day,
>If man's repentance washes guilt away.

In the envoy, Dante bids his song conceal its
inner self until questioned by a friend of virtue,
worthy of receiving its message. This is an excellent specimen of allegory in brief compass.

The other allegory is that of Lady Philosophy.
We have met in the later chapters of the *New
Life* a young girl who, from a window, looks
sympathetically at the afflicted poet, and gradually
awakens in his heart a feeling that he judges to
be disloyal to the departed Beatrice. For this
compassionate lady he wrote several poems —

four sonnets incorporated in the "little book," and probably a few that are not there included. The episode closes, in the *Vita Nuova,* with the triumph of the old love; but the struggle in his heart between two rival interests was presently utilized by him as a symbol of a contest between his placid and religious devotion to the glorified Beatrice and his ardent, impatient, frenzied pursuit of philosophy; and in this second competition it is the new love that for a long time is victorious. We cannot be sure, in every case, whether a poem was intended for the real lady or the allegorical one; and it is evident that when Dante wrote the *Banquet,* he wished his readers to believe that *all* the verses were symbolical, that there never was a sympathetic lady of flesh and blood. The girl of the *New Life,* however, is an uncompromisingly real person; on the other hand, the lady of the odes in the *Banquet,* and of some other poems, has a sufficiently immaterial look to make one suspect her of symbolic intent, even if one had not the author's word for it. At first sight, it seems odd that a very youthful female should have been chosen to represent the majestic science, the "daughter of God;" especially since Dante works out the figure in whimsical detail, making the lady now grand, now sweetly indulgent, now skittish and contrary, now persistently cruel and self-absorbed. We must remember that, in the dejection which followed the death of Beatrice, the poet was comforted at the same time by the pitying face at the window and by the study of philosophy, so that the two were closely associated in his mind; in the *Consolation of Philosophy,* moreover, which Dante was reading just at this time, Boëthius offered a model for a personification of the celestial science as a woman.

Now let us look at three poems which unmistakably belong to the philosophical end of the series, and which are explicitly described by their author as allegories. In the introductory book of the *Banquet* we read, after the definition of the two conditions under which it is proper to speak of one's self: " I am impelled by fear of infamy and I am impelled by the desire of giving instruction which verily no one else can give. I fear the infamy of having followed such a passion as the reader of the aforesaid odes conceives to have ruled over me; which infamy is removed by my present complete account of myself, which shows that not passion but virtue was the moving cause. I intend also to show the real meaning of these poems, which by some cannot be seen unless I tell it, for it is hidden under the figure of allegory. And this will give not only good pleasure to hear, but also subtle teaching, both in that kind of speech and in that kind of interpretation of the writings of others." An allegorical sense, Dante explains further on, " is one that is hid under the cloak of inventions; it is a truth hidden under a pretty fiction: as when Ovid saith that Orpheus with his lyre tamed the wild beasts and made trees and stones come unto him; which meaneth that the wise man with the instrument of his voice doth tame and humble cruel hearts and move unto his will those who have no life of science and art, for those who have no rational life are as stones."

Now, the first *canzone* of the *Banquet*, *Voi che intendendo il terzo ciel movete*, "Ye who by thought the sphere of Venus turn," is an appeal to the angels of the third heaven to listen to the strange conflict that is in the poet's heart, a conflict between his soul, whose comfort hitherto has been the thought of a blessed lady in Paradise, and a new thought, which banishes the old one and assumes dominion over the heart on behalf of a new lady. The frightened soul, weeping and expecting death, is comforted by "a gentle little sprite of love," who tells how wise and kindly is this new queen, and how worthy of reverence. "Song," says Dante, in the envoy, "I believe they will be few who shall understand thy discourse aright, thou speakest it so hard and wearisome" — words which seem to point to a hidden meaning, "a truth hidden under a pretty fiction." In the second of the three poems — a ballad, not included in the *Banquet* — the fiction is still more obvious. It tells of a scornful lady, who, having stolen the poet's heart, will not let him look into her eyes, because she knows that Love is in them, and therefore wishes to keep them for her own enjoyment in her mirror. The third poem (*Amor che nella mente mi ragiona*, the second ode of the *Banquet*) repudiates the sentiments of this ballad, declaring that the cruelty was not in the lady herself, but in Dante's fear of her. Now she reigns supreme over him, as, by God's command, she rules the world. Divine, beautiful beyond words, she reveals the joys of Heaven; and all good thoughts come from her.

In his prose exposition, in the *Banquet,* Dante sets forth as follows the " allegorical and true " meaning of the first of these *canzoni:* " I declare that when the first joy of my soul was lost, whereof mention hath been made above, I was left wounded with such woe that no consolation did help me. Nevertheless, after some time, my mind, which was striving to be well, bethought itself, since neither my own comforting nor another's availed, of returning to the method of self-consolation followed by some disconsolate ones in the past; and I began to read that book of Boëthius, unknown to many, in which, outcast and imprisoned, he had comforted himself; and learning, furthermore, that Tully had written another book in which, treating of *Friendship,* he had uttered words for the consolation of Lælius, a most excellent man, for the death of his friend Scipio, I began to read that. And although it was hard for me at first to enter into their meaning, I finally penetrated it as far as the art of grammar which I possessed, and a little understanding of my own, could go; by means of which understanding I already had discerned, as it were in a dream, many things, as may be seen in the *New Life.* And, as it often happens that a man goeth in search of silver and beyond his expectation findeth gold, presented by some hidden cause, perhaps not without divine command, so I, seeking to console myself, found not only remedy for my tears, but words of authorities and sciences and books; pondering on which, I was assured that philosophy, mistress of these authorities, sciences, and books, was a thing supreme. And I imagined her fashioned as a gentle lady; nor could I picture her in any act save one of mercy. Wherefore did my sense contemplate her verily with such satisfaction that I scarcely could turn it from her. And from this imagining I began to go where she did show herself in very truth, namely, to the schools of the churchmen and the disputations of philosophers; so that in a short time, perhaps in thirty months, I began so to feel her sweetness that love of her drove forth and destroyed every other thought. Wherefore I, feeling myself taken from the thought of the first love to the power of this, opened, as in wonder, my lips to the discourse of the foregoing song, revealing my state under the figure of other things. For of the lady with whom I was falling in love no rime of any vernacular was worthy to speak openly, nor were my hearers sufficiently well prepared to have so easily understood my undisguised speech, nor would their credence have been given to the true meaning as to the fictitious; for it was truly and fully believed that I was inclined to the one love, which was not believed of the other. I began, therefore, to sing: ' Ye who by thought the sphere of Venus turn.' "

Passing on to Dante's greatest and last allegory,

the *Divine Comedy,* we ask: what is the " truth hidden under its fiction; " what, as the author conceived the work, was the " allegorical and true " message he intended to convey? The answer is now not difficult. Evidently, in its fundamental conception, the poem is an authentic confession — in an intricately and symmetrically artistic form — of Dante's recognition of sin, his penitence, and the uplifting of his soul. This is the " truth " concealed under the " fiction " of a journey through Hell, Purgatory, and Paradise — a truth threefold and one, like the Holy Trinity itself. Stripped of its mantle of invention, the real story, the spiritual story, runs thus.

The poet suddenly becomes conscious that he is leading an unworthy life, lost in worldliness. Terrified, he tries to save himself, to change his conduct; but in vain: his vicious habits are in the way. Yet at this very moment the Divine Care which ever watches over men is contriving his salvation; and reason, restored to him by heavenly intervention, comes to his rescue — reason, " faint from long silence." Reason it is that reveals to him in their hideous reality all the vices of humanity, so convincing him of the ugliness, the meanness, the utter folly of sin that he turns his back on it in horror, and by silent, resolute plodding on the upward path leaves it far behind him. But there is more to do. The danger of new temptation is still there; because mankind has by wrongdoing acquired certain perverse tendencies which continually incline it to evil. These tend-

encies are seven in number — the seven cardinal
vices: pride, envy, anger, sloth, avarice, gluttony,
luxury. To some of these Dante is more addicted
than to others: pride, anger, luxury are his besetting sins; but his soul must be absolutely cleansed
of all. There must be no delay; procrastination
is full of peril. The penitent must allow no
occupation — however innocent, however noble
— to impede his reconciliation with God. On the
other hand, the pilgrim who is striving with all his
might suddenly finds himself drawn upward by a
mysterious power not his own. Purity is to be
won only by discipline, submissively accepted from
God's earthly vicar. Hard penance, appropriate
to the fault, cheerfully borne under heavenly
direction, will wash the stain away.

> I would not have thee, reader, be afraid
>   To carry out a good resolve, altho'
> I tell how God demands the debt be paid.
> Consider not the penitential woe,
>   Only the consequence! For at the worst
> Thy pain beyond the Judgment cannot go.

The penance all completed, innocence is restored, and absolute free will: the soul becomes as
guiltless, as joyous, as independent as were Adam
and Eve before the fall. Then it can appreciate,
as never before, God's revelation to humanity, the
redemption of man by Christ, the glory of the
Church, which has triumphantly withstood so
many trials, such deadly assaults from without
and from within. Life is all gladness and beauty.
But the enjoyment of this life is not the highest

reward of moral cleanness. " Blessed are the
pure in heart, for they shall see God." Step by
step the pure soul is led upward by divine revelation. It converses with the blest in Heaven, the
dwellers in the "many mansions" of the "Father's
house." Little by little, as its vision continually
gains in clearness, it comes to grasp the mysteries
of Faith, the wonders of Paradise, the adjustment
of happiness to the capacity of each spirit, the
fulfillment of God's eternal plan. Upward, still
upward soars the pure soul, — now blinded, now
illumined by a brighter light, ever more and more
conscious of the infinite outpouring of divine
Grace, — until it attains its ultimate goal, the predestined end of man, immediate communion with
the Maker. Not through the sense is it conscious
of his presence, not through the understanding,
no longer by means of revelation, but through
direct intuition. No longer does it see " through
a glass, darkly," but " face to face." Such is the
experience that Dante tries, as far as human
speech will permit, to convey to his fellows.

> O Fire Supreme, which human minds ignore,
> Inept to scale thy height, I pray thee, some
> Fragment of thy revealing now restore,
> And lend such power unto mine organs dumb
> That I one single spark of all thy light
> May leave to generations yet to come.
> For if it glimmer on mine aftersight
> And faintly echo in the verse I pen,
> Better conceived by man shall be thy might.
> I think, so keenly did I suffer when
> I faced the living beam, my sight were spent,

CONCEPTION

Had I mine eyes from it averted then.
This thought new courage to my spirit lent,
  As I remember, till my struggling gaze
  On God's immeasurable self was bent.
O grace abounding! thro' the endless rays
  Thou gavest me full confidence to look,
  Till mortal sight was quencht within the blaze.

[From Dante, 372–373.]

LECTURE VII

WORKMANSHIP

IN the Garden of Eden, led by the gentle Matilda, Dante tastes the waters of the river Eunoe, whose sweetness he would fain try to describe, if he had time to linger a little at the close of his *Purgatorio,* the second *cantica* of his poem.

> But since the pages of my second part
> Are filled already, rounding out my plan,
> I am arrested by the check of art.

"The check of art" — a significant phrase. In Dante are united two qualities very seldom mated in one person: spontaneity and discipline. Surely no poet was ever more exuberantly original; yet no other great poet on a large scale has equaled him in severity of restraint, in strict adherence to a preconceived artistic plan. Dante built his *Divine Comedy,* a work of some fourteen thousand verses, with the same system, the same elaborate plotting out, the same subordination of detail to total effect that we find in the formal short lyrics of his predecessors and contemporaries.

Even in the short poem, his patterning, though no more intricate than that of some of his fellow-craftsmen, is carried out with a success, an apparent ease and naturalness, which none of them achieved. As examples let me cite three of his most formal pieces. Here is the opening strophe of one in which the effect depends on the repetition of certain words at fixed points, this repetition taking the place of rime:

O Love, thou plainly canst perceive, this queen
Cares nothing for thy power at any time —
    Thy power, which other fair ones call their queen!
    And when this lady saw she was my queen,
Beholding in my face thine amorous light,
    She made herself of cruelty the queen.
No longer doth her heart befit a queen,
        But some wild beast, whose heart to love is cold;
        For always, be the season hot or cold,
    She governs me as if she were a queen
        Not flesh and blood, but carved in beauteous stone
        By one whose hand is best at carving stone.

And so it runs on through four more stanzas, the same words being used in all, but in an order that changes, according to a set formula, from stanza to stanza. Here is the envoy:

O Song, I carry in my mind a queen
So beautiful, for all she be of stone,
    She gives me courage, tho' mankind be cold,
    To dare to write, despite the season's cold,
        A thing so strange that (by thy constant light!)
        It never was conceived at any time.
[From *The Ladies of Dante's Lyrics*, pp. 78–79.]

The Provençal poet, Arnaut Daniel, whom Dante placed at the head of all writers in the vulgar tongue, had invented a special type of poem in which rime is replaced by repetition. This is the *sestina*, a piece of six stanzas, each of six lines, and, at the end, an envoy of three lines. Throughout the poem, the six lines of all the stanzas end with the same six words; and all six are repeated in the three lines of the envoy. From stanza to stanza their order changes, according to a regular scheme. If the arrangement in one stanza is 123456, the sequence in the next will be 615243: that is, last, first, next-to-last, next-to-first, third-from-last, third-from-first. Dante wrote one poem of this kind, *Al poco giorno ed al gran cerchio d'ombra*, I think the most successful *sestina* ever composed. It belongs, like the one just cited, to the group of poems inspired by that young person whom, for her hard heart, the poet called *Pietra*, or "Stone." Here are the first two strophes:

> Al poco giorno ed al gran cerchio d'ombra
>   Son giunto, lasso! ed al bianchir de' colli,
>   Quando si perde lo color nell' erba.
>   E'l mio disio però non cangia il verde,
>   Sì è barbato nella dura pietra
>   Che parla e sente come fosse donna.
> Similemente questa nuova donna
>   Si sta gelata come neve all' ombra;
>   Chè non la muove, se non come pietra,
>   Il dolce tempo che riscalda i colli
>   E che gli fa tornar di bianco in verde,
>   Perchè gli copre di fioretti e d'erba.

And here is an attempt at a translation of the whole poem:

WORKMANSHIP

To dwindling day and vast encircling shade
   I now have come, alas! and whitening hills,
   When color hath forsook the meadow leaves;
   And yet my longing loseth not its green,
   So rooted is it in the stubborn stone
   Which sentient is and speechful as a lass.
Forever chilly stands this curious lass,
   As snow unchanging bideth in the shade;
   She stirs no more than everlasting stone,
   When balmy spring returns and heats the hills
   And makes them change their hue from white to
      green,
   Decking them o'er with little flowers and leaves.
When that her head is garlanded with leaves,
   One cannot think of any other lass;
   For golden curls so mingle with the green
   That Love is lured to nestle in the shade.
   'T is Love that locks me here 'mid little hills
   Firmer by far than mortar locketh stone.
Her charms more potent are than magic stone;
   She deals a wound incurable by leaves.
   Lo! I have fled thro' plains and over hills,
   Attempting to escape from such a lass;
   But still her light is never screened with shade
   By hillock cast, or wall, or foliage green.
I once beheld this damsel garbed in green,
   So fair, she would have kindled in a stone
   The love I bear unto her very shade.
   Ah! were I with her now 'mid grassy leaves,
   And would that she were fond as any lass,
   Within a field enclosed by lofty hills.
But sooner shall the brooks run up the hills
   Than ever vernal wood so moist and green
   Shall burn (as oft befalls a pretty lass)
   For me, who willingly would sleep in stone
   For all my days, and feed upon the leaves,
   Merely to see the ground her garments shade.

Whene'er the hills project their blackest shade,
Beneath a hopeful green the little lass
Covers it o'er, as stone is hid by leaves.
[From *The Ladies of Dante's Lyrics*, pp. 83–84.]

Another poem belonging to the same group,
one of the most beautifully artistic of Dante's
lyric creations, is the ode *Io son venuto al punto
della rota,* which in its structure exemplifies, as
we shall see, both harmony and contrast. It has
five full stanzas and an envoy. In every stanza
the first nine lines are devoted to a vivid little
picture of some aspect of winter, — the stars, the
atmosphere, the birds and beasts, the trees, the
soil, — while the last four lines affirm and re-
iterate the immutability of the poet's love, insen-
sible to the cold and to the change of seasons.
Antithesis is the basic principle of each strophe;
harmonic symmetry, of the poem as a whole.
Furthermore, the same two opposing principles
are manifested in a recurrent detail, at the end of
every strophe: the last two lines end with the same
word, — *pietra* in the first stanza, *donna* in the
second, *tempo* in the third, *sempre* in the fourth,
dolce in the fifth, *marmo* in the envoy, — but the
sense of the word is always slightly differentiated
in the two lines. Here are two stanzas and the
envoy, as well as I can render them:

The leaves have past their time and had their day,
Which first to life the breath of spring did stir,
To deck the world; no living grass is seen,
And every verdant twig is hid away,
Except on pine, on bay, or else on fir,

Or on some other tree that keeps its green.
The season is so savage and so keen,
The little flowers on the bank it dulls,
Which frost will not endure the earth above. —
And yet unfeeling Love
His thorn from out my bosom never pulls:
Wherefore am I condemned to wear it ever
While I shall live, tho' I should live forever.

The springs pour out their waters mistily,
Pusht forth by vapors hidden down below,
Which mother earth's abysses upward thrust.
The path, on pleasant days so sweet to me,
Is now a running stream, and long shall flow;
For while the winter warreth, flow it must.
Enamel-like the ground puts on a crust;
And stagnant water quickly turns to glass,
Lockt out of doors by petrifying frost. —
Yet I, so battle-tost,
Have not gone back a single step, alas!
Nor will I go! If martyrdom is joy,
Then death must be the best that men enjoy.

Envoy

O Song, what shall become of me when spring
Shall come renewed and sweet, when Love shall fall
Like rain from all the skies to hearts untold,
If now, despite the cold,
Love dwells in me, and nowhere else at all?
I know my fate: to be a man of rock,
If Little Maid shall have for heart a rock.
[From *The Ladies of Dante's Lyrics*, pp. 87–88.]

A subtle example of latent but effective antithesis is offered by the first two stanzas of the first
ode of the *New Life, Ladies who have intelligence
of love.*

Ladies who have intelligence of love,
   About my lady I would speak to you.
   Her praises I can never carry thro';
      And yet discourse of her will ease my mind.
When pondering on her worth, all else above,
   Love steals on me so sweet, I tell you true,
   That, by my speech, to love I then could woo,
      If I had courage, all of humankind.
   But 't is not well so loud a horn to wind
That, terrified, my theme I should forsake:
The verses which I now shall dare to make
      Shall fall her noble merit far behind.
   To you, Love's maids and ladies, I shall sing;
   For no one else is fit for such a thing.

Having thus prepared his readers for a pitiful understatement of the case, our poet forthwith proceeds to launch into the boldest hyperbole ever conceived by mortal mind: Heaven, he declares, is incomplete without Beatrice; the angels feel the lack of her, and beseech God to call her to their company. Here is the next strophe:

An angel in the mind of God doth call
   Saying: " O Lord, on earth there meets our eyes
   A wondrous virtue which doth hither rise
      Forth from a soul whose light doth climb anear."
And Paradise, which lacketh naught at all
   Save only her, unto its Maker cries —
   And every saint — to bring her to the skies.
      Pity alone our earthly plea doth hear;
      For God declareth of my Lady dear:
" In peace, beloved spirits, suffer still
That she for whom ye hope await my will
      Below, where some one her release doth fear,
      One who shall say in Hell: ' O souls distrest,
      Mine eyes have seen the hope of all the blest.' "

In the same book there is another antithesis, which may be called structural, because the arrangement of a considerable part of the *New Life* is based upon it: the contrast between Dante's dream of Beatrice's death and the event itself. The first is told in a long and almost frenzied ode; the second is veiled in silence. The former (the premonition) occurs just in the middle of the story; the latter (the fulfillment), two-thirds of the way along, exactly balancing Dante's conversion to platonic love, which comes after one-third of the narrative.

A much more obvious and violent contrast is furnished by the announcement of the lady's death. After the delirious prophetic *canzone* in the middle of the " little book," we seem to enter on a new phase, a mood of serene, perfect contentment and quiet gladness. First ensues the dainty, playful sonnet of Monna Vanna and Monna Bice, accompanied by the poet's whimsical exposition of the mystic significance of names, and his justification of the figure of prosopopœia — all in a calm and leisurely vein. Next follow two sonnets, *Tanto gentile e tanto onesta pare* and *Vede perfettamente ogni salute,* whose spirit is the very quintessence of peaceful happiness. Then comes a strophe in the same mood, but, if possible, sweeter and more joyous yet, *Sì lungamente m' ha tenuto Amore:*

> So long hath Love possessed me as his own
> And shaped my will unto his mastery
> That, cruel tho' he seemed at first to me,

His presence dear unto my heart hath grown.
And that is why, when all the strength hath flown
From out my breast, and sprites appear to flee,
My fragile soul such sweetness then doth see,
All color leaves my face, save white alone.
Then Love enfolds me with such mighty stress,
He sends my sighs all speechful on their way;
And they my lady pray,
On passing forth, for greater blessedness.
'T is always thus, if she my face behold:
A joy too full of meekness to be told.

And then, immediately after the quiet exaltation
of this last line, strikes in the dull prose, beginning
with a citation from the Lamentations of Jere-
miah: "'How doth the city sit solitary, she that
was full of people! how is she become as a widow,
she that was great among the nations!' I was
still engaged upon this ode, and had finished
thereof the foregoing stanza, when the Lord of
Justice summoned this most gentle lady to glory
beneath the banner of that blessed queen Mary,
whose name was in very great reverence in the
speech of this beatified Beatrice." A low, deep
note, at the very bottom of the emotional scale,
suddenly interrupts the clear, sweet melody, which
was gently soaring to a still higher pitch.

Here we have not only a contrast, but a surprise, as startling as the author's art could make
it. Startling, too, is the climax in the foreboding
vision. In a sick room, where ladies are watching
over him, Dante cries out in his delirium, and,
questioned by the frightened watchers, he consents
to tell his feverish dream. He was brooding, he

says, on his feeble condition and on the instability
of human life, when the thought came to him that
even his lady, being mortal, must perish. At that
he closed his eyes in fear, and, losing consciousness of reality, seemed to see angry women's faces,
which cried: " Thou shalt die! " His story continues thus:

> Then I beheld full many a fearful thing
>   In that delirious, phantom-haunted sleep;
>   And where I seemed to be, I cannot guess.
> I saw disheveled women wandering:
>   Some seemed to shriek, some piteously to weep;
>   Their cries were fiery shafts of mournfulness.
>   Then, bit by bit, the sun, in dire distress,
> Concealed itself, and stars were overhead,
> Appearing tears to shed.
>   Each flying bird came dropping like a flake.
>   The earth appeared to quake.
>   Then came a man all weak and colorless.
> " Have ye not known? have ye not heard? " he said;
> " Your lady, she that was so fair, is dead! "

Surprise is an effect contrived by Dante again
and again, always with great potency, in the
Divine Comedy. Here is an instance. On his
journey through Hell, the author is conversing,
in the circle of the heretics, with the soul of the
great Ghibelline leader, Farinata degli Uberti,
who is standing erect, visible from the waist up,
in a great tomb full of flames. Farinata has just
declared that Dante's ancestors, hostile to him and
to his party, have twice been scattered by him;
and the poet, awestruck at first, has plucked up
courage to retort: " If they were banished, they

returned from every side, both times — an art which your people never learned." At this moment, before Farinata can reply, suddenly appears in the same sepulcher the shade of old Cavalcanti, father of Guido, Dante's first friend.

> Then rose a wraith, uncovered to the chin,
>   Beside the one who first mine eye had caught;
>   I think that he was kneeling there within.
> He stared about my form, as if he sought
>   Some other person who might be with me;
>   But when his doubtful hope had come to naught,
> " If high intelligence thy guide can be
>   Adown this dungeon dark," he weeping cried,
>   " Where is my son? Why comes he not with thee? "

Startling, too, is the incursion of Brunetto Latini. Virgil and Dante are walking along a dike through a desert, amidst a rain of fire. Unexpectedly they meet a band of spirits, disfigured by the burning flakes, hastening in the opposite direction, at the foot of the embankment; and, in passing, each one stares at Dante " as people are wont to stare at one another in the evening under a new moon," knitting their brows, like an aged tailor trying to thread a needle.

> While such a crowd was gazing at me thus,
>   One, recognizing me, let out a cry,
>   Seizing my garment's hem: " How marvelous! "
> And when he lifted up his arm, mine eye
>   His parchèd face went searching thro' and thro',
>   Until the burns no longer could deny
> My eager mind a recognition true.
>   Then, seeking with my face his visage scarred,
>   " You here! " I cried, " Master Brunetto, you! "

WORKMANSHIP

A surprise of a different nature awaits the reader in the meeting of the two travelers with the shade of the poet Sordello, on the slope of the mountain of Purgatory. Virgil, who is puzzled about the path, espies him. " ' But see yonder,' he says, ' a soul all alone, looking towards us. It will show us the quickest way.' We came to it. O Lombard soul, how haughty and disdainful was thy mien, how dignified and slow the turning of thine eyes! It spake not a word to us, but let us go our way, simply gazing, like a lion at rest. Yet Virgil approached it, requesting it to show us the best ascent. The wraith, making no reply to his question, inquired about our country and our life; and my gentle leader was beginning ' Mantua ' . . . , when the shade, which had been all self-absorbed, sprang from the place where it sat, exclaiming: ' O Mantuan, I am Sordello, from thy city!' And each clasped the other in his arms." The episode is invented and thus thrillingly developed by Dante for the purpose of emphasizing the contrast between the love of two departed fellow-townsmen — strangers to each other, and separated by twelve hundred years — and the mutual hatred of fellow-citizens in the Italy of his own day.

There are not a few of these abrupt turns, which affect us like the flash of a meteor. Indeed, Dante himself, in one instance, uses this simile:

As in nocturnal skies serene and pure
  From time to time a spark goes speeding fast,
Startling the eyes which rested all secure,

And seems a star from heaven to heaven cast,
Except that in the quarter where 't is lit
Nothing is lost, and it is quickly past.

Antithesis and surprise are good devices for keeping the reader's interest alert; but our poet had another: suspense. You all know the quiver of excitement, half pleasurable, half painful, that holds you spellbound while a thrilling situation is prolonged on the stage, and the eager expectation that ensues if the outcome is postponed until another act. Some of you have experienced the same sensation in the intervals of a serial story which, in the good, old-fashioned way, breaks off its chapters at tense moments. This emotion Dante knew right well — Dante, who, as he himself more than once declares, was always so keenly inquisitive.

The principle of suspense he uses again and again in his *Divine Comedy,* especially at the close of his cantos. Sometimes it assumes the form of a mere announcement, as when in Heaven the soul of Justinian, wrapped in the effulgence that emanates from its own happiness, is about to answer Dante's questions, " in the fashion that my next song sings."

E così chiusa chiusa mi rispose
Nel modo che il seguente canto canta.

In the ice at the bottom of Hell, two souls are frozen together in one hole, and one of the two is gnawing the back of the other's head. They are Count Ugolino, once ruler of Pisa, and the

enemy who betrayed him, Archbishop **Ruggieri.**
Dante asks him to explain his brutal rage:

> " O thou who showest by such beastly act
>   Hatred for him thy teeth forever bite,
>   Now tell me why," I said, " upon this pact,
> That if against him thy complaint be right,
>   Knowing the names of both, knowing the wrong,
>   I yet shall pay thee in the world of light,
> Unless discourse forsake my withered tongue."

Then the next canto takes up the theme as follows:

> The sinner lifted from its savage grind
>   His crunching mouth, and wiped it on the hair
>   Of t' other's head, which he had spoiled behind.
> Then he began: " Thou wouldst not have me spare
>   My hopeless heart a tale that wakes its woe
>   In very thought, ere language lay it bare.
> But if my words the vengeful seed shall sow
>   Of infamy for this betrayer whom I gnaw,
>   My speech and tears in company shall flow."

Sometimes — once in Purgatory, five times in
Hell — the closing lines of one canto actually
begin the matter that is to form the subject of the
next.

> Meanwhile around the road we circling went,
>   Speaking of things which I must leave behind,
>   Until we reacht the pathway's next descent;
> And there was Plutus, foe to humankind.

Thus ends Canto VI; Canto VII treats of Plutus,
god of wealth, and of the unhappy souls of those
who misused riches.

However, the kind of suspense that I particularly had in mind is something more emotional

than this. An anxious moment is that in which the huge Antæus, at the edge of the pit, lifts up the travelers in his hands and sets them down at the bottom of the well. The terrified poet recalls only the look of the giant as he stooped to pick them up and as he arose after depositing them below. This second posture he likens to the hoisting of a mast into its step, on a ship. The first attitude is compared to the appearance of the Garisenda, one of the leaning towers in Bologna, when the observer is standing right under the slant, and a cloud passes in a direction opposite to the tilt of the tower, making the whole structure appear to be descending on the spectator. " As is Garisenda when you gaze at it from under its slope, while a cloud passes over it in such fashion that it hangs contrarywise, so Antæus looked to me, who was watching to see him bend; and it was an instant when I should have chosen to go by some other road. But lightly he set us down in that deep which engulfs Lucifer and Judas. Nor did he linger thus bent, but rose up like a mast in a ship."

The cold terror that is concentrated in this moment, is in another episode prolonged — namely, in the episode of the opposition of the demons at the gate of the City of Dis, perhaps the most chilling experience of the whole journey. " Above the gates I beheld more than a thousand of the outcasts of Heaven, who cried wrathfully: 'Who is this man who, without death, goes through the kingdom of the dead?' And my

wise teacher made a signal that he would parley
with them privately. Then they suppressed a bit
their great anger, saying: ' Do thou come alone,
and let him go away, who so presumptuously hath
entered this realm. Let him return alone over
his mad path! Let him see whether he can!
For thou shalt stay here, who hast directed him
to this land of darkness.' Imagine, reader, how
hopeless I became at the sound of their accursed
words; for I thought never to return here again.
' O my dear leader,' I cried, ' who more than seven
times hast restored my safety and snatched me
from deep peril that threatened me, leave me not
thus helpless! And if we are not permitted to
pass beyond, let us swiftly retrace our steps together!' And the master who had led me thither
replied to me: ' Fear not; for no one can deprive
us of our passage — it is granted us by such a
Power! But await me here, and feed and fortify
with good hope thy downcast spirit; for I shall
not leave thee in the nether world.' With that,
he departs, my sweet father, and quits me here;
and I am left in doubt, with ' yes ' and ' no ' con-
tending in my brain. I could not hear what was
proposed to them, but it was not long before they
all scuttled back within, at full speed. They
slammed their gates in my master's face, those
foes of ours; and he, left without, turned back
to me with slow steps. With eyes downcast and
brows shorn of all boldness, he said, sighing:
' Who has denied me the houses of sorrow?'
And to me he spake: ' Be thou not terrified, tho''

I be incensed; for I shall win the fight, whatever
be the round of their defense within. This arrogance of theirs is not new. Once they displayed
it at a less hidden door, which still remains without lock. Above it thou didst see the words of
death. Down from it, traversing the rings un-
escorted, is already descending one who shall
open the city for us.' . . . He stood still like
one listening, for his eye could not take him far
through the black air and the thick fog. 'Yet
we must win the struggle,' he began. 'If not —
but think who came! O how I long for some one
to join us!' . . . And he said more, but I recall
it not; because my eye had drawn all my being
to the high tower with the glowing top, where,
in one swift instant, three hellish, blood-stained
furies had arisen. . . . Each one of them rent
her breast with her claws, and beat herself with
her palms, and shrieked so loud that I clung in
fright to the poet. 'Let Medusa come!' cried
all three, staring down. 'Then we shall trans-
form him to stone.' . . . 'Turn back, and keep
thy face covered; for, if the Gorgon shows herself
and thou shouldst see her, there would be no
more returning to the life above.' Thus spake
my teacher; and he himself turned me around,
and, not trusting to my hands, covered my eyes
with his own." At this critical moment a roar is
heard over the waters, like a storm-wind that
sweeps everything before it. "Virgil uncovered
my eyes, crying: 'Now direct thy nerve of sight
over this ancient scum, in that quarter where the

reek is sharpest.' As frogs, at the approach of
their enemy, the snake, all vanish in the water
and crouch upon the bottom, so I saw more than
a thousand dead souls fleeing before one who was
walking over Styx with dry feet. . . . Well I
knew that he was a messenger from Heaven, and
I turned to my master, who made a sign that I
should bow to the visitor in silence. Ah! how
scornful he looked! He reached the gate, and
opened it with a little wand; for there was no
resistance."

On two other occasions Dante is in terror from
demons, and apparently with some reason, although his guide proves to be an adequate pro-
tector. Once, when some devils have actually
succeeded in deceiving Virgil, the poet is dis-
quieted by the indignant look on his leader's face.
"Then my teacher departed with long strides,
his countenance somewhat clouded with wrath.
So I started after . . . , following the prints of
his beloved feet." Thus ends one canto; but
early in the next, "the poultice comes to the
wound:" for "my leader turned to me with that
sweet expression which I first had seen at the foot
of the mountain."

Even in Paradise, Dante is not always free from
apprehension. Peering into the light that envelops the soul of St. John, to see whether, in
accordance with the old legend, the beloved disciple has really been taken up to Heaven in the
flesh (like Christ and Mary), he is stricken with
blindness. "As is a man who stares and strives

to see the sun partially eclipsed, and by seeing
becomes sightless, such I became in the presence
of that last fire; and meanwhile I heard: 'Why
dost thou dazzle thyself to see a thing which hath
no place here? Earth in earth is my body, and
there shall stay until our number shall be equal
to the tale foreordained.'"

> Ah! what a fearful, wonderful surprise!
> For when I turned to look on Beatrice,
> I could not see her form in any wise,
> Tho' near to her, and in the world of bliss!

The following canto, however, once more brings
relief; for Dante is soon assured that his blinding
is only for a little while: "Depend upon it, thy
sight is dazed, not dead."

At the close of Canto XXI of the *Paradiso,*
the poet is alarmed at the outcry of a company of
shining souls on Jacob's Ladder, voicing their
indignation at the degeneracy of modern prelates,
as described by one of their number, Peter
Damian.

> And thereupon I saw, from stair to stair,
> A throng of flamelets, turning, downward flow;
> At every turn their light appeared more fair.
> They joined their mate, and halted there below;
> Then, shouting, lifted up a mighty roar
> Which cannot be compared to aught we know.
> Its thunder stunned me; I could hear no more.

Thus the situation is left until Canto XXII re-
sumes the story. "Crushed with amazement,
I turned to my guide, like a little child who always
runs to her in whom he puts most trust. And

she, — like a mother, who instantly rescues her pale and panting boy with her voice which never fails to soothe him, — spake thus to me: ' Knowest thou not that thou art in Heaven? And knowest thou not that Heaven is all holy, and that whatsoever is done there comes from righteous zeal? . . . From this shout, hadst thou understood its supplication, thou wouldst have learned of the retribution which thou shalt see before thy death.' "

In Purgatory, too, there is a like suspense, and a similar outcry — this time, however, a shout, not of reprobation, but of joyful thanksgiving: a soul (the soul of the poet Statius), having completed its penance, is free to climb to Heaven; and, to celebrate its release, the mountain shakes and all the spirits raise their voices in praise. " We were straining to cover as much of the road as was permitted our strength, when, like something falling, I felt the mountain tremble. A chill came over me, such as seizes a man who is walking to his death. Surely the isle of Delos never quaked so hard, before Latona made her nest in it, to bring forth the twin eyes of the sky. Next began on all sides a shout, so loud that my master stepped close to me, saying: ' Fear nothing, while I keep thee.' All were calling ' Gloria Deo in excelsis,' judging from what I could catch from the souls nearest me, whose cry I could understand. We stood motionless and rapt, like the shepherds who first heard that song, until the trembling ceased and the song was finished. Then we resumed our sacred way, gazing at the souls extended on the ground, who had already returned to their wonted plaint. Never with such sharp attack did any ignorance ever make me crave to know (if my memory in this be not at fault) as that which, while I reflected, now assailed me. But I dared not ask a question, because of our haste; nor could I detect anything by myself. And so I went on, timid and thoughtful." The sequel follows in the next Canto. "That inborn thirst which is never slaked, save with the water for which the woman of Samaria prayed, was tormenting me; and haste was goading me after my leader, over the obstructed way; and pity was pricking me for the punishment, merited though it was. And lo! even as Luke writeth that Christ, already risen from his burial cave, appeared to the two who were on the road, a shade appeared to us, approaching from behind, as we were staring at the prostrate company [of penitent souls]. But we saw it not until it spake first, saying: 'Brothers, God give you peace!' We turned at once; and Virgil replied with a sign that befits such words, and then began: 'May thou be brought in peace into the blessed council by that righteous judgment which sentences me to eternal banishment!' 'What!' cried the stranger, as we walked briskly on, 'if ye be shades that God brooketh not above, who hath led you so far up his stairway?' And my teacher answered: 'If thou look at the marks which the [guardian] angel traces, and which this man beareth [on his brow], thou shalt plainly see that it is fitting for him to abide with the good. . . . I was drawn forth from the broad gullet of Hell to show him the way; and I shall guide him as much further as my teaching can lead. But tell us, if thou knowest, why the mountain gave such shakes, a moment since, and why, even down to its moist feet, all the souls appeared to cry out together.'" Thus Virgil puts to Statius (for the stranger is none other than the spirit just set free) the very inquiry that Dante has been aching but fearing to utter.

> This question thro' the needle's eye did aim
> Of my desire; and so with very hope
> My raging thirst less ravenous became.

Curiosity it is, more than apprehension, that torments the poet, when, on the brink of a well-nigh bottomless cliff in Hell, he is waiting to see what will emerge from the darkness below, in response to a strange signal which Virgil has thrown down into the void. The signal is Dante's belt. " I had a rope girt about me, with which I had once thought to catch the leopard with the painted hide. When, at my leader's command, I had taken it quite off, I handed it to him knotted and coiled. Whereupon he, swinging to the right, threw it down into the deep hole, some distance out from the edge. 'Something curious must surely respond,' I said to myself, ' to the curious sign which my master is so following with his eye.' Ah me! how cautious men should be in the presence of those who not only see the deed

THE POWER OF DANTE

but with their wisdom look into the thoughts! He said to me: 'Soon shall come up that which I expect; that which thy thought is imagining must soon be disclosed to thy sight.' To a truth that hath the semblance of a lie, a man should always close his lips as long as he can, because without his fault it gets him shame. But here I cannot be silent. By the notes of this Comedy, as I hope they be not without long-enduring favor, I swear to thee, reader, that I saw swimming up through the thick, dark air a shape marvelous to the stoutest heart, as one returns to the surface who dives below sometimes to loose an anchor that is caught on a reef or something else hidden in the sea — spreading out at the top and contracted at the feet." What finally does emerge (in the next Canto), after all these preliminaries, is the monster Geryon, embodiment of Fraud and keeper of the eighth circle.

Attentive study of this long preparatory passage reveals a carefully constructed climax, the details being so arranged as progressively to whet the reader's interest: first, Dante's wonder; then Virgil's mysterious hint; next, the suggestion of a thing beyond belief; finally, the impression of impending horror and the vague image of an awful unknown something gradually taking form. Many artistic climaxes could be pointed out in Dante's work, but the unfolding of them would require too lengthy quotation. I shall limit myself to a few obvious cases.

Near the close of each of the three great

[208]

divisions of the *Divine Comedy,* there is a cunningly elaborated scale, leading up to the appearance of Satan, of Beatrice, and of God. As we approach the bottom of Hell, we reach a ring of giants — Nimrod and the Titans — surrounding the mouth of the central well. At the foot of this pit, a lake of ice, imprisoning the souls of hideous traitors. Drawing close to the middle of the round pool, we see looming up in the darkness a form too big and too awful for belief; and a bitterly cold blast sweeps upon us. Our poet takes refuge behind his master, and becomes aware that under his feet, in the ice, are souls in various twisted postures. Suddenly Virgil steps aside, and Dante, full in sight of the monstrous Lucifer, stands shivering, neither dead nor alive. Then follows the description of the three-faced creature.

In the latter cantos of the *Purgatorio* is the lovely picture of the Garden of Eden, fresh with the shade of endlessly varied trees, musical with birds and the rustle of leaves, fragrant with eternal flowers. There, beside the clear, rippling rill, appears, singing and picking blossoms, the figure of Matilda, personification of the charm of youth and innocence. Next comes into sight the majestic pageant of the Church, and in its midst a chariot from which rise a hundred angels, scattering lilies in the air. Through this rain of flowers Beatrice little by little becomes visible. "Ere this I have seen, at the beginning of day, the eastern quarter all rosy and the rest of the sky beautifully clear;

and the sun's face rising so shadowed that,
screened by mists, the eye could bear it a long
time. Thus, enveloped in a cloud of flowers
which rose from angel hands and fell again within
and without [the chariot], a lady appeared to
me . . . clad in the color of living flame." And
Dante, before he sees her face, recognizes her by
the love that floods his heart.

> No further witness was required of sight:
>> By some mysterious power that flowed from her,
>> Once more of bygone love I felt the might.

When Dante, near the consummation of his
journey, emerges from the universe of matter
into the world of spirit, his first impression is of
the boundless, everlasting outpour of divine grace,
which seems like a vast river of light. But this
river presently transforms itself into a round
ocean of golden brightness, about which are
gathered all the blest and the innumerable flutter-
ing host of angels, all illumined by a beam from
above. Accustoming his sight, by degrees, to
all this brilliancy, the poet gradually follows up
this ray with his eyes, until God, the source of
light, is revealed to him.

> O grace abounding! thro' the endless light
>> Thou gavest me full confidence to look,
>> Till quencht within the fire was mortal sight.

[From *Dante*, p. 373.]

In the vision of Satan at the end of the *Inferno*,
of Beatrice near the close of the *Purgatorio*, of
God at the very conclusion of the *Paradiso*, we

find illustrated another structural principle characteristic of Dante's genius, the principle of balance. Furthermore, the figure of Satan, the last thing seen in Hell, is so designed as to balance the conception of God, who is the end and goal of the poet's vision of Heaven. The three Persons of the Holy Trinity — Father, Son, and Holy Ghost, or Power, Wisdom, and Love — have their counterpart in the three faces of the Evil One. The sallow visage on the right, which holds Cassius in its mouth, expresses weakness, the opposite of Power; on the left, the black one, chewing Brutus, signifies ignorance, opposed to Wisdom; the red one in the middle, from whose maw dangles Judas Iscariot, stands for hate, which is contrary to Love. The Devil, looming up in enormous bulk, embedded in ice and rock at the centre of the earth, weighed down by all the pressure of the universe, is inert, save for the flapping of his wings and the crunching of his jaws. The Lord, free from all encumbrance of matter, outside of space and time, is ceaselessly and eternally active, imparting life and motion to the world, sustaining the universe which he has created.

Another balanced pair — though here the relation is less evident — is that of Matilda and St. Bernard, the former symbolizing the highest stage of the active life, a state of innocence and joy, the latter typifying the highest stage of the contemplative life, direct intuition of God. Matilda, a lovely maiden, appears in the Earthly

Paradise; St. Bernard, a venerable elder, in the Heavenly Paradise. Both present themselves to initiate Dante into the mysteries of their respective abodes. Let us look at the two pictures.

Dante, with Virgil and Statius, has been wandering, full of wonder, through the fragrant forest of Eden, and now gazes across the clear, cool stream that bars his progress. "And yonder appeared before me, as sometimes a thing suddenly does appear, which for amazement turns away every other thought, a lady all alone, who walked singing and selecting flower from flower, with which her path was all painted over. ' Pray, fair lady, who dost bask in the beams of love, — if I am to trust to looks, which are usually witnesses of the heart, — be disposed to come forward,' said I to her, ' toward this current, far enough for me to understand what thou singest. Thou dost recall to me what Proserpina was like, and where she was, at the moment when her mother lost her and she lost the springtime.' As a lady, dancing, turns, with feet close to the ground and to each other, scarcely putting one before its mate, so she turned towards me, on the scarlet and yellow flowerets, even as a maid who casts down her modest eyes; and she satisfied my prayer, drawing so near that the sweet music came to me with all its meaning. As soon as she had reached the spot where the grasses were already wet by the ripples of the pretty rill, she granted me the boon of lifting her eyes. I do not believe such light shone beneath the lids of Venus, when she was wounded by her son—quite differently from his habit. She was laughing, erect on the other bank, trailing from her hands variously colored flowers which that high country produces without seed. Three steps apart the stream held us; but the Hellespont, in the place where Xerxes crossed (even now a warning to all human arrogance), did not suffer more hatred from Leander, for swelling between Sestos and Abydos, than this brooklet suffered from me, because its waters did not open then."

For a sight of St. Bernard, we must mount from the Garden of Eden to the mystic white Rose of Paradise. Beatrice, who has been at Dante's side, suddenly vanishes, as Virgil had disappeared in Eden when his mission was fulfilled. The poet turns to question his guide, and sees in her place an unknown figure. " One thing I expected, and another came: I thought to see Beatrice; but what I beheld was an elder, clad like the children of glory. A smiling light of kindness overspread his eyes and cheeks, with a paternal look, such as befits a tender father. And 'Where is she?' I exclaimed. To which he replied: 'To fulfill all thy desire, Beatrice took me from my place. If thou shalt look up at the third tier from the highest row, thou shalt see her again, on the throne which her merits have won for her.' Without answering, I lifted up my eyes, and saw her crowned with a crown of her own making, as she reflected from herself the eternal rays. . . . And the sacred elder spake: ' In order that thou perfectly complete thy journey, to which prayer and holy love have sent me, fly with thine eyes over this garden; for the sight of it will prepare thy vision to mount higher up the beam of light divine. And the Queen of Heaven, for whom I am all afire with love, will grant us every grace; for I am her faithful Bernard.' As one who cometh, perhaps from Croatia, to see our Veronica [the true likeness of the Saviour]; and, having heard of it so many years, cannot look enough, but says in his thought, as long as the image is shown, ' My Lord Jesus Christ, true God, now was thy face indeed like this?' so was I, as I gazed on the living love of him who, in this world, by contemplation tasted that peace."

Symmetry, balance, antithesis, climax — these great architectural contrivances, as we have seen, are abundantly exemplified in Dante's planning, as well as the lesser devices of surprise and suspense. In some cases the suspense is never broken: strange things are purposely left unexplained, and the reader is left to form his own conjectures. This effect of mystery we find most frequently in Hell. On the shore of Acheron, Charon has refused to ferry the poet across, because he is a living man.

> Then suddenly the country dark and drear
> Did quake so hard that memory moisteneth
> My body still with sweat, for very fear.
> The tearful ground sent forth a gusty breath,
> From which a flashing scarlet light did leap,
> Which stunned my senses, even unto death.
> I fell to earth like one who drops asleep.

When he recovers consciousness, he finds himself on the other side, transported we know not how. A little later, as the travelers are circling along the bank of Styx, they come at last to the foot of a lofty tower. " I say, going on with my story, that long before we reached the foot of the high tower, our eyes turned up to its top, because of two little flames which we saw put there; and we saw another returning the signal from so far away that the eye could scarce take it in. Then, turning to the font of all wisdom, I said: ' What does this mean? and what does that other fire reply? and who are the people who have set them?' " These questions remained unanswered.

Mysterious reticence is traditional in oracular utterances. We find it in Dante's rather numerous prophecies. In the real ones — that is, in those which foretell things still in the future when the author wrote — mystery was of course imperative, unless the poet were willing to incur the risk of turning out to be a false fortune-teller. For instance, Dante expected great things of Can Grande della Scala, younger brother of one of the poet's patrons early in his exile, himself a patron toward the end of Dante's life; but as the would-be prophet could not truly know what fate had in store, he had to express his hopes obscurely. In the heaven of Mars, the soul of Dante's ancestor Cacciaguida forecasts the poet's exile, his sojourn with the Lombard family of la Scala, his first acquaintance with Can Grande, then only nine years old, and the mighty deeds which this future hero is destined to do. " ' Wait for him and his kindnesses. By him many people shall be shifted, rich and beggars exchanging conditions. And thou shalt bear away written of him in thy memory, but thou shalt not tell — ' And he told me things unbelievable even to those who shall see them."

Skilful restraint often suggests more than any explicit discourse could impart. Suggestion, conveying the impression of something far beyond the power of words, is one of the finest tools of our poetic craftsman; and with an example of its use I shall conclude this account. He employs it especially in the *Paradiso,* where he has to do with things outside the world of the senses. "Henceforth," he declares, "my language, even in that which I remember, shall be briefer than that of a babe that still wets its tongue at the breast." "Oh! how short and weak is speech," he cries, "compared to my idea! And even that, compared to what I saw, is such that 'little' is all too insignificant a word." Gazing on the beauty of Beatrice, enhanced as it is by her approach to her heavenly home, he exclaims:

> If what hath e'er been said of her could all
>   Combine into a single praise and blend,
>   For this occasion it would be too small.
> The beauty now before me doth transcend
>   Not only human thirst: the Infinite
>   Alone can drink it to the very end.
> This test hath found me wanting, I admit,
>   Far worse than any one of poet kind
>   Was ever vanquished by his hardest bit.

WORKMANSHIP

E'en as the sun the feeblest eye doth blind,
   E'en so the sweetness of her smile doth chase
  Itself from memory, leaving naught behind.
Since first in mortal life I saw her face
   Until I saw it thus supremely blest,
  My song hath constantly pursued her trace;
But now my fond pursuit must come to rest —
   Pursuit of loveliness in poesy —
  Like every artist who hath done his best.

LECTURE VIII
DICTION

Apollo, pray, for my remaining task,
   O! make me such a vessel of thy might
   As they must be, for laurels dear who ask.
Till now, enough has been a single height
   Of old Parnassus; now I need the two
   To succor me in this, my final flight.
Enter my bosom now, and breathe anew,
   As when from out the scabbard of the skin
   Thy conquest Marsyas' bleeding body drew.
O power divine, let me thy favor win
   Until to tell the blessedness I see
   Fading from memory's chambers, I begin.
Then shalt thou see me seek thy favorite tree
   And crown myself with thy beloved bay,
   Made worthy by my subject and by thee.
So seldom, Father, is it pluckt to-day
   (O shame upon the base desires of men!)
   To decorate or victory or lay,
That joy should swell in joyous Delphi when
   The leaf that keeps immortal Daphne's name
   Awakes the hankering of poet's pen.
A tiny spark may light a glowing flame;
   And after me a louder prayer may rise,
   And Cyrrha's echo may repeat the same.

With this impassioned supplication to Apollo, or heavenly inspiration, Dante launches upon his tale of Paradise. At the beginning of his *Pur-*

gatory, too, he prays for help, this time from Calliope, genius of poetic art:

> The second realm of spirits I shall sing,
>> Where penitent the soul itself doth shrive
>> And thus prepares its heavenward way to wing.
> But now be Poetry, sunk in death, alive,
>> O holy Muses! I am in your care.
>> And let Calliope a bit revive,
> And play, in harmony with me, that air
>> Which Pieros' wretched daughters once did hear
>> So grandly swell, it drove them to despair.

As we read the divine poem, we seem, from time to time, to hear the strumming of the Muse,

> As skilfully guitar accompanies
>> A skilful singer, with its quivering string,
>> And thus the song hath double power to please.

> E come a buon cantor buon citarista
>> Fa seguitar lo guizzo della corda
>> In che più di piacer lo canto acquista.

With the tinkle of the harp and the guitar, we hear the tinkle of the morning bell which the clock rings:

> And as the clock, which early summons all
>> And wakes the Church, the Bride of God above,
>> To woo the Bridegroom with her matin call —
> The clock, where push and pull the wheels that move,
>> And *ting-a-ling* so musically sing,
>> The quick responsive spirit swells with love:
> Thus I beheld revolve the glorious ring,
>> Voice answering unto voice, in perfect peace
>> And sweetest concord, past imagining,
> Save yonder, where delight can never cease.

Indi come orologio che ne chiami
   Nell' ora che la sposa di Dio surge
   A mattinar lo sposo perchè l'ami,
Che l'una parte l'altra tira ed urge,
   Tin tin sonando con sì dolce nota
   Che il ben disposto spirto d'amor turge:
Così vid'io la glorïosa rota
   Muoversi, e render voce a voce in tempra
   Ed in dolcezza ch'esser non può nota,
Se non colà, dove gioir s' insempra.

The clock was still a thing new and strange enough to be a source of pleasurable wonder. Rings of souls, dancing around at greater and less speed, are compared to wheels in clockwork:

Just as the wheels that regulate a clock
   Revolve so different, to the watchful eye,
   One flying seems, one still as any stock.

I have quoted all these passages, not so much because they speak of harmony as because by their sound and suggestion they create it. Artistic balance, harmony of sound, of phrasing, of sentiment: that is the secret of the pervasive, soothing charm of Dante in his gentler moments.

What then I heard imprest me like the thing,
   The very thing that always strikes the ear
   When organs play and people stand and sing,
And now we lose the words and now we hear.

Tale imagine appunto mi rendea
   Ciò ch' io udiva qual prender si suole
   Quando a cantar con organi si stea,
Ch' or sì or no s'intendon le parole.

DICTION

Thus it is when we read Dante for the first time — indeed, even for the twentieth time: the meaning of the words now is plain, now elusive, but the majestic music of the verse sounds on like a mighty organ, suggesting things beyond our present ken.

> And thence, as cometh to the listening ear
> Sweet harmony from organ pipes, there comes
> Before mine eyes the time that draweth near.

> Da indi sì come viene ad orecchia
> Dolce armonia da organo, mi viene
> A vista il tempo che ti s'apparecchia.

These are the words of Dante's ancestor, Cacciaguida, in the sphere of Mars. In this same Heaven of Mars, the shining souls of innumerable Crusaders, grouped in a gigantic Cross, all join in one sweet, distant song, a song whose loveliness transcends human understanding:

> As harp or viol, tuned to harmony
> Of many strings, doth tinkle sweet and shy
> To one who catches not the melody,
> Thus from the lights appearing in the sky
> There swept along the Cross a strain of song
> That baffled sense, but lifted me on high.

> E come giga ed arpa, in tempra tesa
> Di molte corde, fa dolce tintinno
> A tal da cui la nota non è intesa,
> Così dai lumi che lì m'apparinno
> S'accogliea per la croce una melode
> Che mi rapiva senza intender l'inno.

[221]

Kindliness it is which bids these spirits interrupt their hymn, that Dante and Cacciaguida may meet and hold converse together.

> It bade that dulcet lyre its music cease,
> And stilled those holy strings, which Heaven's hand
> So dextrously doth tighten and release.

> Silenzio pose a quella dolce lira,
> E fece quïetar le sante corde
> Che la destra del cielo allenta e tira.

Silence just as sudden falls upon St. Peter, St. James, and St. John, whose dazzlingly bright spirits have been singing and circling about the poet:

> Stopt sudden at the word the fiery round,
> And stopt the concert sweet they made together
> (Three spirits breathing forth harmonious sound),
> As, at the threat of weariness or weather,
> The oars that rhythmic cut the sea before,
> When boatswain pipes, all hold themselves in tether.

> A questa voce l'infiammato giro
> Si quïetò con esso il dolce mischio
> Che si facea del suon del trino spiro,
> Sì come, per cessar fatica e rischio,
> Li remi, pria nell'acqua ripercossi,
> Tutti si posan al sonar d'un fischio.

A mighty choir singing in unison we have heard in Mars, a harmony of three voices in the starry firmament; now let us listen to a soloist with a choral accompaniment, compared to a soul that shines bright against the gleaming orb of Venus:

[222]

DICTION

As spark within a flame is plain to see,
  As voice within a voice is plain to hear,
  When one is still and one doth flit and flee,
Thus lights within the brightness did appear,
  With different swiftness circling — I believe,
  According as their heavenly sight is clear.

  E come in fiamma favilla si vede,
    E come in voce voce si discerne,
    Quando una è ferma e l'altra va e riede,
  Vid' io in essa luce altre lucerne
    Moversi in giro più e men correnti
    Al modo, credo, di lor viste eterne.

The harmony that continually resounds in Dante's Heaven is, of course, a symbol of the spiritual harmony of the blest. Every soul sees God in its own way, each enjoys its own degree of beatitude — some higher, some lower, but all content, and all together forming one vast celestial symphony of happiness. "Now I see," exclaims the poet, "how everywhere in Heaven is Paradise, although God's grace doth not descend equally on all." The heavenly concord and the heavenly joy — joy complete to the utmost capacity of each soul — naturally express themselves in music:

Within the ones that first to meet me came,
  Hosanna rang so sweet that since that hour
  I ceaselessly have longed to hear the same.

  E dentro a quei che più innanzi appariro
    Sonava *Osanna* sì che unque poi
    Di riudir non fui senza disiro.

THE POWER OF DANTE

The angel Gabriel sings, flying like a ring of light
about the Blessed Virgin:

> The sweetest tune we hear on earthly shore,
> Which closest draws the soul it doth inspire,
> Would seem a rifted cloud's tempestuous roar,
> If likened to the music of that lyre.

> Qualunque melodia più dolce suona
> Quaggiù, e più a sè l'anima tira,
> Parrebbe nube che squarciata tuona,
> Comparata al sonar di quella lira.

The vowel coloring in many of Dante's lyrics,
and in some of the episodes of the *Commedia*
(notably that of Francesca da Rimini), beautiful
as it is, is too subtle to be analyzed. It does its
work, but the reader knows not how nor why.
The effect can be consciously appreciated only
after frequent reading aloud. It can be more
easily caught in short snatches, such as those
which I have quoted, or such as the following:

> Io venni in loco d'ogni luce muto,
> Che mugghia come fa mar per tempesta,
> Se da contrari venti è combattuto.

> I reacht a spot where every light is dumb;
> It bellows like the sea tempestuous,
> When blown by blasts which there to battle come.
>
> [From *Dante,* p. 299.]

The key-note is given by the *u* in *luce, muto,
mugghia, combattuto,* suggestive of the low roar
of the storm-wind, and reinforced by the *m* of
muto, mugghia, mar, tempesta, combattuto.

[224]

Io venni in loco d'ogni luce muto,
  Che mugghia come fa mar per tempesta,
  Se da contrari venti è combattuto.

In another passage, the echoing rumble of a distant waterfall sounds like the hum of a beehive:

Già era in loco ove s' udia il rimbombo
  Dell' acqua che cadea nell' altro giro,
  Simile a quel che l'arnie fanno rombo.

In the following translation, having at my disposal no such effective words as *rimbombo* and *rombo,* I have distributed the reverberative suggestion:

Now we had come where we could hear the drum
  Of echoing waters tumbling down below,
  Which rumbled like the busy beehive's hum.

More subtle is the impression of the following lines, telling of the swift departure of some shining souls, which, like rapid sparks, "veiled themselves with sudden distance"—a wonderful figure, which I shall not attempt to reproduce in verse:

E quasi velocissime faville
  Mi si velar di subita distanza.

The sparkle of the *i* in "velocissime fav*i*lle m*i* s*i*" . . . fades into the deep *a* and *u* of "vel*a*r di s*u*bita dist*a*nza."

Another factor in Dante's suggestiveness is the repetition of words fraught with associations of the mood which the author wishes to induce:

for instance, in the Francesca passage, the abundance of such tender and sad terms as *amor, amar, amante, dolce, piacer, pace, dolore, doloroso, lagrimar* wonderfully enhances the emotional impressiveness of the story itself.

> Amor, che a nullo amato amar perdona,
> Mi prese del costui piacer sì forte
> Che, come vedi, ancor non m' abbandona.
> Amor condusse noi ad una morte.

In a very different strain is the sonnet in which the poet regrets having wasted his rhetorical efforts on an impervious female — perhaps Lady Philosophy, perhaps a woman of flesh and blood — and emphasizes his impatience by repetition of the angry word *maledico,* " I curse." " I curse the day when first I saw the light of your treacherous eyes, and the moment when you came to the crest of my heart to pluck the soul from it. And I curse the loving file, the polisher of words and pretty metaphors, which I have invented and set to rime for you, to make the world honor you forever more. And I curse my stubborn memory, which is sure to keep that which is destroying me — your beauteous and cruel face, for whose sake Love is often condemned. Wherefore doth everyone laugh at him and me, who hope to rob Fortune of her wheel."

> Io maledico il dì ch' io vidi im prima
> La luce de' vostri occhi traditori
> E 'l punto che veniste in cima
> Del core a trarne l'anima di fuori.

E maledico l'amorosa lima
  C'ha pulito i miei detti e i bei colori
Ch' io ho per voi trovati e messi in rima,
  Per far che il mondo mai sempre v'onori.
E maledico la mia mente dura,
  Ch' è ferma di tener quel che m'uccide:
Cioè la bella e rea vostra figura,
Per cui Amor sovente si spergiura;
  Sicchè ciascun di lui e di me ride,
Che credo tor la rota alla Ventura.

Whatever regrets Dante may have felt about
his " loving file, the polisher of words and pretty
metaphors," we surely need feel none. The metaphors and similes that his file has polished to perfection constitute perhaps the most obvious attraction, not only of his lyrics, but still more of his
Divine Comedy. One could dwell long on this
branch of his art; but, as it does not strictly belong
to the present subject, I must content myself with
a few specimens. There is a graceful comparison
(used later by Boccaccio) in Dante's ode *Tre
donne intorno al cor mi son venute.* One of the
three allegorical ladies rests her face in her hand,
drooping " like a plucked rose."

Dolesi l'una con parole molto
  E 'n sulla man si posa
  Come succisa rosa;
Il nudo braccio, di dolor colonna,
Sente l'oraggio che cade dal volto.

One lady, answering in tearful wise,
  Doth face on hand repose,
  E'en as a severed rose;
Her bare supporting arm, pillar of grief,
Doth feel the shower that falleth from her eyes.

THE POWER OF DANTE

Just now we were speaking of bees. They were not the only insects that the poet recognized: in one passage he refers to the hour of dusk as " the time when the fly gives way to the mosquito." The busy ant claimed his attention; and the curious trait he records is one that he evidently had observed for himself: two companies of spirits, passing each other in opposite directions, and kissing as they go by, seem to him

> Like ants within their dusky regiment,
> Each member touching noses with his mate,
> Perhaps to ask his luck, or whither bent.

The frog finds a place in Dante's collection. Some of the damned, nearly covered by ice at the bottom of Hell, suggest the frog, who, " in the season when the peasant woman often dreams of gleaning, seats himself, with his muzzle out of the water, to croak." These we have already met, and likewise the frogs who " scatter at the hostile snake's approach," and all " crouch on the bottom."

Of bird life the *Divine Comedy* is full, the poet's favorites, among feathered creatures, being falcons, cranes, and doves. Here is a procession of lost souls, borne through the air by the blast of Hell, like a long flight of cranes:

> And as the cranes, with doleful ditty, surge
> Along the air, in lengthened streamer lined
> Thus coming saw I, uttering their dirge,
> Souls ever carried by the self-same wind.

DICTION

We see the hawk released from its hood, shaking its head and flapping its wings as it prunes itself, revealing its eagerness to be off; the young stork, which, impatient to fly, lifts its wing, but lowers it again, not daring to leave the nest; the daws, which, at daybreak, begin to flutter all together, to warm their chilly plumes, as is their habit, some flying away for good, some returning to their starting-point, others wheeling constantly about.

As Dante was ever disposed to look upward, he watched the stars quite as lovingly as the birds. Now he gives us a picture of the sky after sunset, when the stellar lights begin faintly to appear.

> When evening first begins to climb the blue,
>   New objects slowly show themselves on high,
>   And what we see seems true and yet untrue.

Now a host of souls first speaking in chorus with one mighty voice, then singing individually, is compared to the sun, shining by day with a single light, and after nightfall reflected in a host of stars.

> When he who, turning, all the world doth light
>   Descends below and quits our hemisphere,
>   And sunshine everywhere gives way to night,
> The sky, erstwhile with his effulgence clear,
>   Is suddenly restored to view again
>   By many lamps which, lit by him, appear.

Now a bright angel, approaching over the sea, looks, to the observer on the shore, like Mars shining close to the horizon:

[229]

We still were motionless upon the shore,
  Like people wondering about their way, —
When body stops, but heart goes on before, —
And lo! as often ere the break of day
  Mars through a mist sends forth a ruddy light
  Down in the west, above the level bay,
Thus (as I hope again to see that sight!)
  A gleam came speeding o'er the sea so fast,
  Its swiftness went beyond the quickest flight.

The ocean furnishes many beautiful effects. "The mortal sight of your world," says Dante, "can penetrate eternal justice no more than your eye can fathom the ocean; for although the eye discern the bottom from the shore, it sees it not on the main; yet the bottom is there, hidden by its depth." Embarking on the tale of his journey through Purgatory, he begins:

At last the little vessel of my mind
  Doth hoist its sails to cross a better sea,
  Leaving that cruel ocean far behind.

At the outset of Dante's description of Heaven, we find a majestic figure:

O ye who, following in little boats,
  Eager to hear, have come so long a way
  Behind my ship, which singeth as it floats,
Go back and seek your shores while yet ye may!
  Tempt not the ocean! Haply were ye lost,
  If, losing trace of me, your craft should stray.
The sea I enter never yet was crost.
  Minerva sends the wind, Apollo steers,
  Nine Muses chart the stars of polar frost.
Ye others, few, who turned in early years
  To eat the holy bread that angels keep,

> Which feedeth men, but always scant appears,
> Well may ye venture on the salty deep,
> If but your skiff run close upon my wake
> Before the sea resumes its level sleep.
>
> [From *Dante*, pp. 231–232.]

We may conclude our brief survey of metaphors, or rhetorical colors, with this picture of a
storm:

> Already swept the turbid waters o'er
> The turmoil of an uproar full of fright,
> Which made a shiver run thro' either shore.
> Its course was like a furious storm-wind's flight,
> By heat and cold at odds made over-strong,
> Which unobstructed doth the forest smite;
> The boughs it strips and breaks and spins along.
> Forward it fares in all its dusty pride,
> And beasts and shepherds run, a fearful throng.

You may have been surprised, in the first of
my quotations to-day, to hear an invocation of
Apollo and the Muses by the foremost of Christian poets. Theologians were apt to regard the
pagan deities as devils, fallen angels, who had
beguiled men to worship them. Dante himself
seems to have interpreted in this fashion some of
the figures of ancient mythology, especially those
associated with the lower world. Others, like
Apollo and the Muses, were for him mere poetic
abstractions. Jupiter represented the heathen's
vague conception of the Godhead. Some of the
ancient divinities, such as Venus, were invented,
he thought, to explain the influence of the stars.
"The world," he says, in the *Paradiso*, "used to
believe, to its peril, that the fair goddess of

Cyprus radiated mad passion, as she revolved in the third epicycle. Wherefore the people of old, in their old error, not only did honor to her, with sacrifice and votive shout, but they honored Dione [her mother] and Cupid [her son]; and they went so far as to say that he sat in Dido's lap. And from her, with whom I begin this canto, they took the name of the star which is wooed by the sun, now before, now behind." The story of Cupid, disguised as Ascanius, sitting in the lap of Dido, is told by the wise Virgil himself.

We do not know just how far Dante thought that Virgil and Ovid actually believed in the supernatural tales they told, how far they considered their divinities and their narratives to be mere allegorical and rhetorical inventions. At any rate, he felt himself quite free to use the mythological apparatus without compunction, with no more fear than had Boileau, in the seventeenth century, of being called a pagan. When occasion required, he altered the semblance or the character of the traditional figures, giving Charon, for instance, rings of fire around his eyes, and making Cerberus, with his three mouths, the embodiment of vile gluttony. Plutus, god of riches, is turned into an inflated, clucking hobgoblin, which, at Virgil's speech, collapses into a helpless heap. "As wind-puffed sails, when the mast snaps, tumble in a tangled pile, so dropt to earth that cruel beast." The kingly Minos, who after death became a judge of departed souls, is transformed by Dante into a demon with a long tail, which he

winds around and around himself in such a way
as to indicate the stage of Hell to which each soul
is condemned. "There sits Minos horrid and
snarling; he examines the sins at the entrance,
judges and sentences according as he coils. I
mean that when the ill-born soul comes before
him, it confesses everything; and that expert in
evil, determining what part of Hell befits it,
girdles himself with his tail as many times as the
steps down which the spirit is to go."

Not very literally, then, did Dante take the
mythology of the ancients. To the poets, whom
he regarded as enlightened beyond other men,
he was inclined to attribute some inkling of religious truth, which, from time to time, shows
dimly through their fables. Thus, when the
Latin sages wrote of the Golden Age and the
original innocence of mankind, they may have had
a vague concept of the Garden of Eden and the
state of Adam and Eve before the fall. So says
Matilda, the beauteous keeper of the Earthly
Paradise, through which she is leading Dante with
Virgil and Statius. " ' Those poets who of old
sang of the Golden Age and its happy state, perhaps on their Parnassus were dreaming of this
spot. Here it was that the human stock was
innocent; here is the eternal springtime, here is
every fruit. This is the nectar, whereof they all
tell.' At that, I turned all the way around and
faced my poets; and I saw that they had received
her last sentence with a smile."

Not content with the traditional poetic mythology, the allegorizing Middle Ages cherished a sort of intellectual, prosaic mythology of their own. For example, the seven planetary heavens, which by the ancients had been turned into gods and goddesses, we find expounded by Dante, in the *Banquet,* as symbols of the seven liberal arts, Grammar, Dialectics, Rhetoric, Arithmetic, Music, Geometry, and Astrology. The sky of the fixed stars stands for Physics and Metaphysics. The ninth and last revolving heaven, the Crystalline, which envelops all the rest of the material universe, signifies Ethics. The Empyrean, or heaven of spirit, the real Paradise, represents Theology. Now the third among the planetary spheres is that of Venus, the fair Goddess of Cyprus, of whom we were speaking but a moment ago; and her heaven is the symbol of the third liberal art, which is Rhetoric. " The heaven of Venus," explains Dante, " may be compared to Rhetoric, on account of two properties : one is the clearness of its face, which is pleasanter to see than any other star; the other is its appearance now in the morning, now in the evening. And these two properties are to be found in Rhetoric. For Rhetoric is more pleasing than any other science, because that is its principal purpose. It appears in the morning, when the rhetorician speaks before the eyes of his hearer; it appears in the evening, when the speech is made by the rhetorician at a distance, in writing."

The rhetorical authorities most respected in the Middle Ages were Aristotle and Cicero, both of whom are cited by Dante. In the thirteenth century not only Rhetoric but also Dialectics and Logic had come to the fore in the universities. Possibly the study of Rhetoric strengthened the natural leaning of the Middle Ages toward impersonality in writing, and maintained that tendency even in an author of such powerful individuality as Dante. Perhaps, if he had never studied Rhetoric, he would have left us, in his two spiritual autobiographies (the *New Life* and the *Divine Comedy*), some account of his material life. As it is, he never mentions his children, his wife, his brother; of his parents he says only that they spoke Italian; there seems to be in one passage of the *Vita Nuova* an indefinite reference to one of his two sisters. That is all he has to say of his immediate family. Of the events of his career there is scarcely more. "It is not admitted by the rhetoricians," he states, "that anyone may without necessity speak of himself." The reason, as he goes on to explain, is that we cannot speak of ourselves without either praising, which is unbecoming, or blaming, which is still more shameful. Petrarch, in theory, had the same views; for in one of his letters he declares: "I leave aside domestic matters, about which you wrote me at some length, inasmuch as they are not worthy of being treated in a noble style." On the whole, it is likely that Dante got from his poring over rhetorical problems more benefit than detriment, although it is hard to believe that the conscious, studied workmanship is in the *Divina Commedia*

a more effective factor than the spontaneous, sub-
conscious artistry. Still, it is quite impossible to
separate these two, in Dante or in anyone else.
Whether he would, without the pursuit of Rhetoric, have written a better or a worse poem, we
cannot say. At any rate, no one would wish it
different.

"I declare," says the author of the *Banquet,*
"that the *goodness* and the *beauty* of any discourse are distinct and different from each other.
For the goodness is in the meaning, and the beauty
in the ornateness of the words, both being de-
lightful, although the delight of goodness is
greatest." "The ornateness of the words"
seems to be Dante's definition of what was generally called "eloquence," an art frequently discussed by the scholars of his time. In the fourteenth century a favorite subject of debate was the
question whether Cicero or Virgil was the more
eloquent writer. Petrarch, in one place and another, has much to say about poetry; and nearly
all the things he says could just as well be said
about prose. What he and his contemporaries
most appreciated in prose and verse, from an
æsthetic point of view, was this same eloquence.
Dante's treatise on versification in the vulgar
tongue is named *De Vulgari Eloquentia,* "On
Vernacular Eloquence." Eloquence is the idiom
of poetry; but it is also the idiom of prose. What
it means essentially is *style.* "Our beloved
Cicero," wrote Petrarch, "is beyond doubt the
father of Latin eloquence. Next to him comes

DICTION

Virgil; or, perhaps, since there are some who dislike the order in which I place them, I had better say that Tully and Maro are the two parents of Roman literature." The failure to make any clear distinction between prose and verse style we find again, centuries later, in some of the Neo-Classicists.

(The illustrious vernacular, declares Dante, is to be used in prose as well as in verse; but in verse it has to be employed with more originality, because prose writers naturally copy their predecessors.) We may perhaps assume that poetry demands a higher degree of eloquence. But even in verse there are several grades: in the subjects that suggest themselves we must use judgment in deciding whether they are to be sung tragically, comically, or elegiacally. " By tragedy," he says, "we mean the higher style, by comedy the lower, by elegy we understand the style of the wretched. If things seem worthy of being sung tragically, we must take up the *illustrious vernacular,* and consequently construct an *ode.* But if they are to be sung comically, the middling, sometimes the lowly vernacular is to be assumed. . . . But if they are suited to elegiac song, only the lowly vernacular must be used. However, let us pass over the others; and now, as is fitting, let us deal with the tragic style. We may be said to use the tragic style when the majesty of the lines, the high quality of the construction, and the excellence of the words harmonize with the gravity of the subject."

[237]

This, then, is the highest degree of poetic eloquence: a combination of elegant versification with choice vocabulary. This is the " tragic style." It is to be noted that, to Dante's generation, the words *tragedy* and *comedy* generally conveyed no idea of drama: they signified respectively noble and familiar composition and, at the same time, tales with unhappy and with happy endings. *Tragedy* was used especially to designate a story of the downfall of a great personage. *Comedy,* therefore, may naturally indicate an account of a rise from low to high estate. Dante's great poem was called by him a *Commedia;* the epithet " Divine " was added by admiring posterity. And he called it a *Comedy* by reason both of its style and of its subject. At least, so we are told in the Epistle to Can Grande, which is probably what it purports to be, an authentic letter of Dante to his patron.

It is likely that Dante seized with alacrity upon the distinction between tragedy and comedy, in order to fortify himself with a reason for using in the *Divina Commedia* whatsoever style suited the moment, instead of maintaining the language at a constant pitch of monotonous eloquence. This elevation he had to sustain, as a matter of course, in his regular odes; but what can advantageously be done in a poem of a few stanzas may well be quite impracticable in a lengthy composition. Virgil, to be sure, kept up the noble tone throughout the *Æneid;* that work, however, was written in *grammatica,* or Latin, in which eloquence is easier.

Nevertheless Virgil was, in fact as well as in the fictitious journey, Dante's guide and master. At the beginning of the *Hell*, when, after vainly attempting to pass the three beasts which bar his way up the mountain, Dante is falling back into the depths, there appears before him a shape that looks " faint from long silence." Seeing this form in the midst of the great waste, he calls out: " Have pity on me, whatever thou be, shadow or real man."

> Quand' io vidi costui nel gran diserto,
>   " Miserere di me," gridai a lui,
>   "Qual che tu sii, od ombra od uomo certo!"

Virgil replies: "Not a man; I was a man once, and my parents were Lombards, Mantuans both by birth. I was born under Julius Cæsar, though late in his rule; and I lived in Rome under good Augustus, in the time of false and lying gods. I was a poet, and sang of that just son of Anchises who came from Troy, after proud Ilium was burned. But thou, why art thou returning to such distress? Why dost thou not climb the delectable mountain which is the source and cause of all joy?" Overwhelmed at finding himself face to face with the great master, "'Now art thou that Virgil, that spring which spreads abroad such a wide river of eloquence?' I replied to him with brow abashed. 'O honor and light of other poets, let me reap the reward of my long study and of the great love that hath made me seek out thy book. Thou art my master, my model. From thee alone

did I derive that beauteous style which hath won
me honor.' "

> " Or se' tu quel Virgilio, e quella fonte
> Che spande di parlar sì largo fiume? "
> Risposi lui con vergognosa fronte.
> " O degli altri poeti onore e lume,
> Vagliami il lungo studio e il grande amore
> Che m' ha fatto cercar lo tuo volume.
> Tu se' lo mio maestro e il mio autore;
> Tu se' solo colui da cui io tolsi
> Lo bello stile che m' ha fatto onore."

" That beauteous style which hath won me
honor: " just what did Dante mean by " beauteous
style "? Some critics have thought he meant the
proper choice of words, some have suggested that
what he had in mind was allegory. It is to be
observed that Dante is referring to a benefit already enjoyed, for he says, "Lo bello stile che
m' ha fatto onore," " the beauteous style which
hath won me honor; " therefore he must be speaking, not of the *Divine Comedy,* which he is just
beginning, but of works previously published and
applauded, particularly, no doubt, his odes, written in the tragic or higher style. Let me repeat
Dante's definition of that style: " We may be said
to use the tragic style," he says, " when the majesty
of the lines, the high quality of the construction,
and the excellence of the words harmonize with
the gravity of the subject."

The phrase "majesty of the lines," *superbia
carminum,* undoubtedly signifies a preponderance
of eleven-syllable verses; for the author himself

says, a little further on: " Of all these lines, the eleven-syllable is manifestly the most majestic, both in the time it consumes and in its capacity for meaning, construction, and vocabulary." By " the high quality of the construction," *construc-tionis elatio,* he seems to mean periodic sentence-structure, which, he declares, is favored by the use of the long eleven-syllable line. The third factor, " excellence of the words," *excellentia vocabu-lorum,* or choice diction, is also, in his opinion, best cultivated in the long line. Now, of these three elements, it was presumably the third, " excellence of the words," that gained most from Virgil's example. His influence may have been consider-able, also, in the second, "high quality of con-struction;" and even in the first, "majesty of the lines," his use of the hexameter may have been one cause of Dante's preference for the longest Italian verse that he knew. In this definition there is no place for allegory. Of course Dante attached the highest value to allegory, and regarded Virgil as a great allegorist; but, although he employed allegory in some of his odes, he probably did not include it in the phrase *bello stile.* In his discourse on allegory, in the *Banquet,* Dante cites as a secular example, not Virgil, but Ovid. Neverthe-less, when he came to construct the symbolic frame-work of the *Divine Comedy,* it was Virgil rather than Ovid that he followed.

I said that the words " the beauteous style which hath won me honor " must refer to Dante's past writings, not to the crowning one which is just at its inception. This does not mean that Virgil's influence ceased, or that it is less conspicuous in the great poem than in the smaller ones. Quite the contrary is true. Having found the master's teaching so profitable in his lyrics, Dante follows it still more clearly in his grand *Commedia*. Over this the genius of the *Æneid* most unmistakably presides. If we consider the "majesty of the lines," we find that in the *Comedy,* not only most of the verses, but virtually all, are of eleven syllables. As for "high quality of construction," the periods in the *Comedy* are, on the average, more fully rounded, ampler, and more supple than those of the odes. With regard to "excellence of words" the superiority of the long poem in Virgilian quality is most striking: whereas the odes reveal in their choice of words only the general Virgilian principle of fitness and elegance, the *Comedy* displays in countless passages a direct borrowing of vocabulary, as well as of metaphor and incident, from the *Æneid*. Dante had, then, good reason to love and revere Virgil as a friend and teacher.

> "Poet that guidest me," I then did say,
> "Consider well my strength (can it suffice?)
> Ere thou consign me to the mighty way."

After Virgil has stilled his disciple's doubts, we hear the cry of readiness and trust:

> "Thy words so potently my heart have bent
> With eagerness my journey to pursue
> That I return to this, my first intent.

Now go! a single will is in us two.
Thou guide, thou lord and master!" Thus I pray.
And when he forward stept, my leader true,
I entered on the deep and woody way.

" Tu m'hai con desiderio il cor disposto
Sì al venir con le parole tue
Ch' io son tornato nel primo proposto.
Or va', chè un sol volere è d'ambedue:
Tu duca, tu signore e tu maestro."
Così gli dissi; e poi che mosso fue,
Entrai per lo cammino alto e silvestro.

Dante's feeling toward Virgil is reflected in the
attitude of the Latin poet Statius, whose shade,
just released from penance, is met during the passage upward through Purgatory. His art and
inspiration, he avers, even his reform and conversion and consequently his salvation, he owes to
the *Æneid* and the *Eclogues*. The *Æneid,* " that
divine flame which hath illumined more than a
thousand," was his " mother and nurse in poesy."
It was a sentence in this poem that first made him
aware that prodigality, to which he was addicted,
is a sin, and thus led him to correct himself. It
was a prophecy in the fourth Eclogue that first
opened his eyes to Christianity. All this he tells to
Virgil himself, whose identity he does not suspect.
Then he exclaims:

" Could I have lived when Virgil was alive,
My just completed term of banishment
For one full year I gladly would revive."
Virgil, at this, his gaze upon me bent
With lips that in their silence said: " Be still! "
But human will is not omnipotent;

THE POWER OF DANTE

For smiles and tears so instantly fulfill
  The hest of every feeling whence they flow,
  In truthful men they least obey the will.
I smiled, like those who secret knowledge show.
  The shade stopt short and lookt me in the eyes,
  The eyes, which best reveal the heart below.
" Now, by the outcome of thy great emprise,
  Say why, erstwhile, as I thy visage scanned,
  My glance a flash of laughter did surprise."
Now am I caught on one and t' other hand:
  One calls for silence, t' other calls for speech!
  I heave a sigh; my Sage doth understand:
" Fear not," he saith to me, " the truth to teach.
  Speak boldly and divulge, at my behest,
  What Statius doth so earnestly beseech."
Wherefore I said: " Perhaps thou wonderest,
  O ancient spirit, at my laughing face.
  With greater wonder thou shalt be imprest!
This shade, which upward guides my mortal pace,
  Is Virgil, in whose verses thou hast found
  The power to sing of gods and human race.
If thou my laugh didst otherwise expound,
  Give up thine explanation as unmeet.
  The speech of Virgil was the real ground."
Swiftly he bowed to clasp my leader's feet;
  But Virgil cried: " O brother, do not bend!
  For thou art shadow; shadow thou dost greet."
He rose and said: " Now canst thou comprehend
  The greatness of mine ardent love for thee,
  When I to shadows fleshly substance lend,
Forgetting our unbodied vanity."

[From *Dante*, pp. 344–345.]

To the personage of Statius our poet probably
ascribed some of his own traits, and much that he
here puts into the mouth of the ancient Latin
surely represents Dante's own sentiment and ex-

perience. His regret at not having been a contemporary of Virgil is spoken in this instance by Statius; but he himself indirectly expresses the same thought when he cries out in sorrow, on finding that his guide has left him. It is in the Garden of Eden, and Dante, absorbed in the contemplation of Beatrice, whom he has just recognized, turns impulsively to communicate his great joy to his master; but discovers that he is gone. The poet's face, which has been washed clean with dew, is again stained with tears, despite all the charms of Eden — Eden, once sacrificed by mother Eve. "I turned to the left, with that expectation with which the little boy runs to his mother, when he is frightened or in trouble, meaning to say to Virgil: 'Not a drachm of blood is left in me which is not a-quiver. I recognize the tokens of the old fire.' But Virgil had left me bereft of him — Virgil, sweetest father — Virgil, to whom I gave myself for my salvation. And all that our ancient mother threw away could not prevent my dew-cleansed cheeks from turning dark again with tears."

Only in imagination can Dante consort with Virgil. What a comfort, what a delight would have been his companionship in the flesh! But Virgil's place is among the dead, Dante's among the living. And not even after death can the disciple meet the master; for the one is destined to dwell in Heaven, while the other, a pagan, must forever dwell below. All this, I think, is implied in the brief parting. If Dante, like Petrarch, had hit upon the idea of writing letters to the dead, he surely would have addressed an epistle to the poet whom he so cherished; but he had not that solace.

Before Virgil departs, however, he bestows upon Dante an assurance of proficiency, a solemn declaration that the 'prentice, now become a master, needs no other direction than his own will. Of course the reference is to the conduct of Dante's spiritual life; but the words may be applied in all truth to his stylistic training and graduation. "The temporal and the eternal fire hast thou seen, my son," says Virgil, — that is, the fire of Purgatory, which is but for a season, and the fire of Hell, which lasts forever; "and thou art come to a place where I, by my own effort, can see no further. I have led thee hither by wit and art. Now take thine own pleasure as guide. Thou hast emerged from the steep paths and from the narrow ones. Behold yonder the sun, which shines upon thy brow; see the new grass, the flowers, the shrubs, which the soil here produces of itself. Until those beauteous eyes, — which, weeping, moved me to come to thee, — shall come in gladness [until Beatrice shall come to seek thee], thou mayest sit and walk amidst them. No longer await my word or my sign. Free, upright, and whole is thy will, and it would be wrong not to follow its judgment. Wherefore I crown and mitre thee over thyself [I make thee thine own emperor and pope, arbiter of thy worldly and religious life]."

[246]

DICTION

E disse: "Il temporal fuoco e l' eterno
   Veduto hai, figlio, e sei venuto in parte
   Dov' io per me più oltre non discerno.
Tratto t' ho qui con ingegno e con arte;
   Lo tuo piacere omai prendi per duce.
   Fuor sei dell' erte vie, fuor sei dell' arte.
Vedi là il sol che in fronte ti riluce;
   Vedi l' erbetta, i fiori e gli arbuscelli,
   Che qui la terra sol da sè produce.
Mentre che vegnan lieti gli occhi belli
   Che, lagrimando, a te venir mi fenno,
   Seder ti puoi e puoi andar tra elli.
Non aspettar mio dir più, nè mio cenno:
   Libero, dritto e sano è tuo arbitrio,
   E fallo fora non fare a suo senno;
Per ch' io te sopra te corono e mitrio."

Here we have indeed an admirable specimen of
the "bello stile." The lines are not only "majestic," but grandly rhythmical and full of subtly
charming assonances (such as " E fallo fora non
fare a suo senno "). The " quality of construction " is as high as Dante can make it: the sentences are built with exquisite balance, fluent and
perfectly clear, each complete in its own tiercet;
of the sixteen clauses, half show the typical prose
order, half show a normal rhetorical inversion;
nowhere is there anything like unnatural dis-
tortion, nowhere any evidence of the constraint of
verse. The words are excellently sweet, both in
their sound and in their connotation; the line
" Fuor sei dell' erte vie, fuor sei dell' arte,"
" Thou hast emerged from the steep paths and the
narrow ones," shows an ingenious play on the
words *erte,* " steep," and *arte,* " narrow," this

[247]

latter being a pure Latinism. At the close we
have in rime the dignified and impressive *arbitrio*
and *mitrio*. Let this example of our poet's
" beauteous style " be our parting word. After
this speech, the best I can do is to leave you alone
with Dante.

Await my word no more, for here I halt.
    Free-willed your judgment is, and just and true;
    To follow not its faith would be a fault.
Your crown and mitre shall be worn by you.

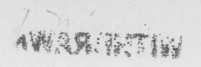